I GOTTA GO

The Commentary of Ian Shoales

A PERIGEE BOOK

Perigee Books
are published by
The Putnam Publishing Group
200 Madison Avenue
New York, NY 10016

Library of Congress Cataloging-in-Publication Data

Shoales, Ian, date.
I gotta go.

1. United States—Social life and customs—
1971–   —Anecdotes, facetiae, satire, etc.
2. American wit and humor.   I. Title.
E169.02.S484   1985   973.92   85-16914
ISBN 0-399-51177-6 (pbk.)

Printed in the United States of America
1   2   3   4   5   6   7   8   9   10

ACKNOWLEDGMENTS

Many of these commentaries first aired on National Public Radio's *All Things Considered* and ABC's *Nightline*. Some of them have been rewritten slightly to replace the strident tones of the spoken word with the measured cadences of thoughtful prose. Some have been written especially for this collection. They all appear here in print for the first time.

Any similarity with persons real, living or dead, is accidental. Mr. Shoales wishes to offend real people, not capture them in print.

Does Mr. Shoales wish to thank anybody? No.

Contents

CONTENTS

CONTENTS

CONTENTS

INTRODUCTION

BY JOE THE BARTENDER

This guy Ian Shoales comes into my place a couple, three times a week. I say he's got a big mouth, but he says he's a social critic. I say if you're so important, bub, why don't you pay the 47.50 you owe me. He says no problem I got a book coming out, the movie rights alone will pay for the bar tab. Well I trust this guy about as far as I can throw him. So then he butters me up. He says to me would I do an introduction to his book.

Well my idea of a good read is Louis L'Amour or one of those Robert Ludlum deals, but I figure what the hell. This guy wants me to introduce him, all right, and if this thing ever gets to paperback I can show it to the kids and they'll think the old man is a deal.

So he says he's on radio and TV (I'm going, "Sure you are.") and he wants to introduce his unique world view to a reading audience. So, okay, I listen to his tapes. He talks real fast—so as to get the full impact of what he has to say, you better read fast, I guess. Between you and me and the fence-post, this Ian Shoales ain't no Mickey Spillane. He's more like one of those guys on television that don't necessarily reflect the views of the management and staff. Most of the stuff he wrote in here I heard him saying to anybody who would listen in the bar.

So you want to know what this guy is like? Okay, in conclusion then.

1. He drinks two mugs of ale when he comes into the joint. One about nine and the other about 12:30. He tries to get people to buy them for him.

2. He sure is skinny for sitting around so much.
3. He likes to play "Heartbreak Hotel" on the juke as many times as I will let him. Other of my patrons have complained about this.
4. If somebody plays Barry Manilow he kicks the jukebox. I have had to ask him to leave on several occasions because of this type behavior.
5. He owes me 47.50.
6. Buy this book so he will pay me my 47.50.

Joe
3/1/85

I GOTTA GO

FOREWORD

Messages on the Fridge

The Fridge The American refrigerator: in the '50s it was a squat white thing, rounded at the edges. The chrome trademark glistened in the fluorescent light. It was a Buck Rogers dream come true. It made *modern* home a *home*. Forget Bauhaus, forget the entire history of architecture and interior design. Forget the slave-driven pyramids and Christ-centered cathedrals. The Fridge erased it all.

Kids invaded the Fridge for cookies and milk. Mom hovered around the Fridge as if afraid it might suddenly vanish. Dad avoided the Fridge. The Fridge was never empty of cold things. I'd come home at 4 A.M., and no light would shine but the old Kelvinator light, spilling out on the faded linoleum. The cold Fridge was the warm center of the house, even in the deadest of night.

The door of the Fridge was covered with yellowed coupons, or jokes from *Reader's Digest* ("Humor in Uniform," "Life in these United States") or *Saturday Evening Post*. The *Post* joke page haunts me still: those sexless gremlins rolling in hysterical convulsions on the cartoon ground. The door held shopping lists, letters from Grandma, newspaper clippings, inspirations, thoughts, poems, phone numbers—all this paper held in place by Scotch Tape turned brown by the sun. The door of the Fridge was so thick with paper you couldn't see the surface anymore. I'd come home from school, see the open window, sun streaming in, the thick layer of refrigerator paper swaying and crinkling in the spring breeze. The Fridge was the communications center of America. Everything I know about America I learned from the Fridge.

The Amazing Two-Headed Dog I remember best a mysterious photograph of a Russian scientist posing grimly with a two-headed dog he'd created in the laboratory (clipped from _Life_, naturally). I would stare at it for hours as I munched thoughtfully on my Oreos. Why would a Russian scientist put two heads on a dog? Would an American put two heads on a dog? No. Americans give cancer to white mice. Why do Americans give cancer to white mice? So Americans won't get cancer. So does a Russian scientist put two heads on a dog so Russians won't get two heads? What did this picture _mean?_ Did it mean that not even Rover was safe from the cruel machinations of godless communism? Was it a warning to America that we were falling behind in the two-headed dog race? It was a complicated world.

I realize Mother was trying to teach me about the world, but the combination of Fridge information and data gleaned from grade school was much more input than my young gray cells could take. My fifth-grade teacher, Miss Norgaard, would herd us into the furnace room, which did double duty as fallout shelter and screening room. There, by the furnace, we saw scratched grainy images obtained from the U.S. Information Service, projected onto a cinder-block wall. On that wall we saw Russia for what it was: a grim hard world (no Batman, Popsicles or refrigerators) filled with stubby treacherous men with machine guns, all crouched behind the Iron Curtain. These film strips and black-and-white movies showed us a _cartoon_ Iron Curtain, but never told us where it was.

When Iron Curtain headlines showed up on the Fridge, or when Huntley and Brinkley talked about the Iron Curtain, I always pictured a small overstuffed and overheated parlor, divided in half (East and West) by a small iron curtain. It had the same consistency as steel wool, with a faded-pink floral pattern. On their side fat men swapped guttural secrets in a foreign tongue. On our side a handsome American agent knelt (either Efrem Zimbalist, Jr., or Jack Kelly), trying desperately to decipher what the fat men were saying. And that flimsy

Iron Curtain was all that kept Boris from waddling in America's back door and taking away the Motorola, the hi-fi, all that kept godless Soviets from drawing thick black censor's lines through the messages on the Fridge.

I was shown words and concepts constantly, but nobody told me what they meant. What were guerrillas in Hungary? Starving apes? Poor anthropoids kept from a balanced meal by stubby men with machine guns? What was a cold war? Was it cold as Russia's heart? Cold as lemonade? Was it cold because it was a war of words and talking kept you warm? When my mother put the clippings in place of Khrushchev banging his shoe, Mother's fear didn't rub off on me. After all, here was a guy who just wanted to go to Disneyland. These images were pieces in a puzzle I had no desire to solve: banging with a shoe, threats in a bizarre language, mushroom clouds, the *Life* version of World War II versus the cartoon version, in which it seemed that the Pacific War was won single-handedly by Popeye.

This collision of cultural images didn't bother grown-ups. They dragged me to church, dragged me to visit maiden aunts. I stood in tight shoes, politely listening to dull conversations, struggling to stay awake as aunts and uncles in faded parlors muttered about their gas pains and operations. Was this world worth defending from the Reds? I understood that I was supposed to think so, but I didn't understand the world of grown-ups, and I sure as hell didn't want any part of it, or Russia either. They both seemed like the same world to me.

Russians all seemed to look like my Uncle Frank—fat, with a shiny suit a size too big, with huge gaps between large yellow teeth. Every time he came to visit, Uncle Frank would give me a Batman comic, then steal it back when he left. He gave me dutch rubs, and expected me to do something cute if he gave me a dime. I wasn't afraid of Uncle Frank exactly, but I can't say I looked forward to his visits either.

And every President we've had in my lifetime reminded me of my Uncle Donald. Uncle Donald would insist on taking me to football games, even though I've always hated football.

(Football players, like prostitutes, are in the business of ruining their bodies for the pleasure of strangers.) For birthdays Uncle Don gave me baseball caps and argyle socks, when what I wanted were Batman comics, Johnny Horton records, and hightop sneakers. My kindly uncle was giving little Ian what he thought little Ian needed, not what little Ian wanted.

All right, this is a fifth-grade view of politics, but don't blame me, blame the Fridge. Who is more stupid—their world leaders who want to go to Disneyland, or our world leaders who won't let them. Sure, I didn't want the Commies to take my comic-book collection to Siberia. After all, I had the original *Spiderman*. I still have it. It'd be worth a couple thousand if I still had all the pages. It was a comic-book world back then—bold Yankees versus heartless Reds. But now I want to read comic books, not live in them.

Into the Gap If comic books were one of the glories of American life, why didn't my mother want me to read them? Stern warning about comic books would appear on the Fridge, from half-baked Freudian quacks, would-be Abbies and Sister Anns. And, as I got older and my hair longer, the messages got stern and hysterical—articles about hippies who took LSD and went blind staring at the sun, stories about rock-and-roll–ruptured eardrums. Around 1966 (the year I got my first record player—it folded up like a suitcase and made a fascinating and incredibly annoying fuzzy warble when you jacked the volume all the way up), the Fridge stopped being a communications center at all, and became Propaganda H.Q. for the older side of the generation gap. The messages became adult screams across the '60s canyon—no dialogue, no discourse, no more *Hints From Heloïse*, no more "Three Cents Off on Lux," just pictures of mud at Woodstock (from *Life*, naturally).

Of course, my parents were right. Woodstock *was* miserable. I knew it would be. That's why I didn't go. But my parents missed the point. It was fun *because* it was miserable. Woodstock was one of those "Reach out and Touch Someone" memories so awful it seems wonderful in retrospect. Certain events are not fun as they occur, but leap into the memory with a curious fondness. Memories like that keep you humble. They make you realize you're just a sap like everybody else. We're all just saps on this planet, but we can do something about it. If you go through life as a sentimental jerk you deserve everything that happens to you. Nostalgia about Woodstock made the Us Festival possible, the B side of the pop-culture disc, an event that disappeared in the mind as soon as you ticked off the names of rock stars you glimpsed dimly through binoculars. The Us Festival is just a clone of fun, an encyclopedia of this year's models. MTV is hardly better, but at least there you get attractive women dressed like high-heeled Nazis. It's time to face the music, kids. The '60s are over.

Remember the words "Made in Japan"? When I hear "Made in Japan" I remember the prizes pulled at age ten from "Guess What?" boxes, or "Crackerjack." These candies were the bane of dentists but the delight of a small boy with contempt for healthy teeth. I hunched in a dark movie house, my teeth glued together, my eyes glued to Audie Murphy on the silver screen, as I removed my Japanese prizes from the candy boxes—a fortune-telling fish (a piece of red fish-shaped cellophane that would always wind up on the Fridge), instructions for a magic trick that never worked. (These wound up on the Fridge.) None of these prizes (each clearly marked "Made in Japan") ever worked, so how in the '80s am I supposed to believe that the words "Made in Japan" are symbols of quality in workmanship and design? Every time I see the words "Made in Japan" I think of Audie Murphy, not personal computers. It's not Japan's fault—after all, they gave us Kurosawa movies and sushi—no, it's me getting caught in the vile clutches of *nostalgia*, the world's most useless emotion.

The other day I was flipping the AM dial, when some Golden Oldies format spun a stupid 45 from 1966. I won't sully the page with the name of this song, but let me tell you the same trite melody that made me throw my radio out the window twenty years ago, now brought tears of remorse. I remembered *everything:* where I was when the song was playing, which girlfriend had just given me the heave-ho. This silly insipid song put heat on my cheeks, and pain in my heart. But then I wised up: this was left-over pain, not a connoisseur's sorrow. Cupid's dart may hurt like death when you're very young, but the quivers pack a tiny sting today. Nostalgia is to memory what aspirin is to penicillin—it's just an easy sugar-coated pill to swallow, and it doesn't cure old pains; no, nostalgia just brings symptoms—self-pity without irony, regret without wisdom.

The '60s Are Over   We don't have to pretend to hate our parents anymore. We don't have to be ashamed if we work for a living. We don't have to pretend to admire Hermann Hesse or Richard Brautigan. We don't have to pay attention to Abbie Hoffman or Jerry Rubin. We don't have to endure endless guitar solos. We don't have to feel like some kind of jerk because we don't want to yell obscenities in the face of a cop with a loaded gun. We don't have to go to protest meetings and listen to every faction give its side until everything's so politically correct that nothing gets done, except to make sure the leaders' names are spelled right in the college newspaper, thus assuring them continued coverage when they become liberal lawyers, or minor literary figures with books called *The Use of Poetry in the Classroom* (as if poetry were *functional* and, as such, subject to laws—that's Brain Police talk; we have enough cops, we don't need them watchdogging the culture).

You can throw away your Norman Mailer and Joan Didion. We're grown-ups now. I'll say it out loud. William Burroughs is *no fun;* his dreary books read like scrambled messages from Mars. Timothy Leary *is* from Mars. He's on the lecture circuit with G. Gordon Liddy, for God's sake. We're well into the '80s now. Boors and yahoos are yahoos and boors no matter what political fence they straddle. We can think for ourselves. And unless you gobbled LSD like candy like certain friends of mine (God rest their brains), you don't have to treat every thought that enters your head with reverence and gratitude.

I remember back in 1967 arguing with my girlfriend's mother about Vietnam. All the argument got me was a firm order never to set foot in her house again, until I got a haircut. Or a job. Or joined the Army. So I never saw my girlfriend again. And the War went on.

Dad kicked me out of the house for the last time in 1968, and Mom began *sending* me the clippings she once put on the Fridge: friends who got married, friends who got good jobs, and (in recent years) friends who died.

I get more like my parents every day. It's hard to stay hip over thirty. I find myself agreeing with Joe Friday when I watch *Dragnet* reruns. You have to work hard to maintain interest in a stereo component system. Digital, laser disc—who can keep up? It's hard to afford speakers as big as my bed. I sleep on a Futon, but if I had a queen-size mattress I'd have to get speakers that big, I have an obligation. I'm a social critic.

I gotta do something when I hear the music of the '80s. Gotta stay on top of what's going down, get hip to what's hot. This might mean grabbing my shades and my snap-brim hat, borrowing somebody's Porsche to swing by the 7-11 to see if the new *Rolling Stone*'s hit the stands yet. It might mean watching Cable TV twenty-four hours a day. It's hard to pay attention to America, and America wants attention so *badly*.

Maybe the Age Of Aquarius will come after all, and we'll all gather around the *cappuccino* together, hicks and sophisticates, morose feminists and fat Republicans, to write in our journals and discover our innermost thoughts. Maybe guys and gals will think from the right half of the brain at last, and stand in the clear white dawn of a new day as spotless as Tom Wolfe's Sunday suit. But I doubt it.

Where's My Pulitzer?   This might be astonishing prose, but where is it taking us? I've tried to talk to yesterday's pop stars about the future of America. I called Linda Ronstadt to ask, "You've worked with Nelson Riddle, what does he think about music in the '80s? Does Frank Sinatra hate reporters as much as he says he does?" She hung up on me. My only reply was the dial tone, that persistent whine that's been scientifically proved damaging to both hemispheres of the brain. They can split up AT&T, but they still can't destroy the dial tone. This tells me something.

What are things coming to, when fading pop stars won't take a meeting with a guy like me, a guy on the cutting edge of the new wave, a guy who's trying to get people out of the sound track of their own mind movies, into the clear south-of-the-border light you only see in films by Sam Peckinpah? Sure, I'm tired of reviewing popular culture—it's no occupation for a grown man—but I can't go back to old-wave thinking. The Fridge is gone forever, along with macrame, thin women with big guitars, decoupage, and wah-wah pedals. I am what I am, over thirty at last, but still a teenager in circular time (not linear time), a teenager with a brain.

I've made my peace with the folks. We play Scrabble together, as I listen to the Ramones on my personal stereo system. My folks talk to me about retirement, I talk to them about the hot new groups on the Coast. They live in a warmer climate now, untouched by the Cold War, with a sharp-edged fridge that matches their pastel condo kitchen. They've got a microwave and no more messages at all.

I live alone. My fridge is a small efficiency job I read about in *Apartment Life*. There's just enough room for yogurt and a six pack, enough freezer room for a plastic tray of ice cubes, none at all for a turkey pot pie. But sometimes, when I'm feeling like a sentimental jerk, I buy some white bread and Velveeta and make myself a sandwich, just the way Mother used to make it in the Cold War days. Then I remember détente and Watergate, feed the whole mess to the neighbor's dog, crack a cold one, and think about where America's heading.

If you've got any ideas about the future of America, keep them to yourself. I mean it. Or write a note about it and put it on *your* Fridge. Don't send it to me. I don't even want to hear about it. I don't have time to listen to your advice. I'm too busy giving my own: Watch your hearts, pals and gals. If you cruise down memory lane, drive carefully. Wear your seat belt and don't leave your brains at home—most of the memories on memory lane are merely nostalgia; and nostalgia is just a memory that was made in Japan. All right, now, let's get on with the book.

At Joe's, 3/1/85

NATION

Fear

Somewhere in the fifties William Powell and Myrna Loy stopped dancing the rhumba till dawn, and Manhattan became the Naked City. The Concrete Jungle buried The Thin Man. And somewhere in the seventies the Concrete Jungle became a Charles Bronson movie. The clash between civil liberties and "traditional values" (whatever that means) has created what *Time* Magazine likes to call "a climate of fear."

All that this means is: the movies changed. The climate of fear ain't the weather I live in. The gun isn't my umbrella.

And isn't fear one of the reasons we move to the Big City in the first place? As a hick with urban pretensions I know I moved to the city for the romance—writing hard-edged prose in a garret, having a painfully thin girlfriend, and friends who wear berets and only shave every three days. As a younger man I welcomed my fears, which were mundane enough—Where is the rent coming from? How will I eat? Is anybody paying attention to me? What if people start to take me seriously, what will I do? Will I ever publish that 1,500-page rock-and-roll novel that doesn't quite fit in the sock drawer?

As far as real fear goes, yes, the streets are unsafe, full of intense confrontations, the ravings of street people, the desperate poor, and hardened criminals, but I don't see how subway showdowns will solve anything. Juvenile delinquents and vigilantes would love to live in a city where they can take pot shots at one another as they dodge down the mean streets. But they shoot straighter in the movies. In real life innocent people get in the way.

How can the government help? Is it really the job of government to second-guess the actions of potential psychopaths?

What do we want? A personal armed guard? A SWAT team at every stop? These things cost money, you know. Most Americans would rather live in mortal terror than pay more taxes.

Nowadays if you see a couple in a tux and mink you don't say "Hiya Nick and Nora," you mutter "rich jerks" under your breath and move along. I miss *The Thin Man* as much as anybody, but if you can't stand the heat, go live in a Jimmy Stewart movie. New York ain't Smallville, folks. Archie and Veronica don't live in the Big City. If The City was a nice place to live, nobody would live there.

On the Muni, 1/19/85

The Unexplained

These are modern times, the New Age, the Computer Age, the Age of New Technology, but the old mysteries still surround us. Think of all the stories—the tales of UFO's, of the Bermuda Triangle, of psychics and poltergeists, of exorcists and terrorists. . . .

The blind albino alligators in the sewers of New York; the woman in Texas who never washed her beehive do, so a spider made its nest in it; the poodle that exploded in the microwave. . . .

The ghosts: phantom hitchhikers; phantom truckdrivers; the ghost of Paul McCartney on *Abbey Road*. . . .

The homicidal maniacs: the killer's hook in the handle of the door; the boyfriend's body thumping gently on the roof of the car; the frat pledge found on the mansion roof after the initiation, his hair white, his eyes insane, tapping the roof with a bloody hammer. . . .

The sinister conspiracy that killed the Kennedys; the babysitter's discovery that the killer was in the house with her.

All the old teenage werewolves and Frankenstein monsters have grown into '80s adults. Think of the scary images thrown at us—the Jolly Green Giant, Mr. Clean, Man from Glad, the Welchkins, E.T., Muppets, The alien, the Thing, Care Bears, Cabbage Patch dolls, even Betty Crocker and her mysterious bland omnipotence in the American kitchen.

Think of the tiny destructions of video games: apocalypse and rejuvenation for a quarter. Think of the power of coins: the images of dead presidents engraved on rare metals; the seeing eye of the pyramid on the dollar.

And think of real terror: punk's power to shock and society's power to turn shock into glamour; Edie Sedgwick, Andy Warhol, Sid Vicious, Jayne Mansfield, Charles Manson; society's misfits and monsters. Think of Christ's face on a taco, Elvis glimpsed in a vision, falling hunks of Skylab, radioactive Russian satellites; think of Baby Fae, think of the Heart Men. . . .

We've got the bomb for good now. The old black magic is still afoot, in our dreams and deeds, the gods and demons are not dead. And the Bogey Man'll get *you*. If you don't watch out.

After reading Pet Sematary, *11/30/85*

The Beef

Fast-food chains are full of political figures: Mayor Mc-Cheese, Colonel Sanders, Burger King, the court jester Jack-in-the-Box, even Wendy, the token woman. Fast-food chains seem to be a cute little community inside the larger national community, where *everybody's* friendly and happy, the memories are as golden as the french fries, and your car will be towed if you linger longer than twenty minutes over your lunch.

That's all right, that's lunch in the fast lane, but now, in political cartoons, headlines, even in debates, the phrase "Where's the beef?" has stampeded into our political vocabulary as one more layer in the sandwich of media clichés. I suppose "Where's the beef?" was cute when first uttered in the fast-food commercial (if you think commercials are cute) and I suppose that a red-blooded American finds strength in red meat—a strong man is a *beefy* man; we *beef* up our foreign policy; we put *beef* behind our law enforcement—but here's *my* beef:

"Where's the beef?" does not cut the mustard as an in-depth probing political question. When you ask a candidate "Where's the beef?" what's he supposed to say? "The beef is in my foreign-relations policy," or "Oh, the beef? That's in my strategic-arms-limitation scenario." And if our next President is the man with the beef, will that endear him to our allies? Can a President say to a summit meeting, "Hey everybody! I've got the beef! Now you listen to me!"?

If we must have a commercial catchword to define our discourse, I recommend, "Gee, your hair smells terrific!" Walk up to President Reagan and say, "Gee, your hair smells terrific," and he'll say, "Thanks, yours does too," and you've got a conversational gambit that will get the ball rolling. But ask the President "Where's the beef?" and he and his advisers might spend the next few hours searching frantically for raw hamburger in the pockets of his three-piece suit.

Americans should comparison-shop for fast food and Presidents. After all, we want a President who's as strong as a good cup of coffee, but won't keep us up at night; a President who gives us more miles to the gallon, but still has room for the entire family; a President who isn't hazardous to the national health.

But remember, a President lasts for four years, and lunch only lasts twenty minutes (before they tow your car away). As you cruise down the strip looking for our next President, look for the bright neon of issues, the real meat of political ideas. Who do you want for President anyway? Ronald McDonald? Don't say Burger King, pals and gals. After all, this is a republic.

Off the campaign trail, 1/22/85

Fast Food

Every time I go to McDonald's, and I go there about once a week, I try to imagine America without fast food. Fast food has become a necessity, like cars and telephones. I sip my tepid shake, chew my cold fries and double cheeseburger, and try to understand what I'm doing—am I eating or shopping? The commercials make McDonald's seem like a place where lovers meet, where families gather, where memories leap into being like the magical appearance of a ghost or an old friend. We're supposed to remember going to McDonald's the same way we remember going to the prom or the occasion of our firstborn. But they're just Hollywood images, not real. The memories blur into one large pleasant, fuzzy image. Those endless bags of fries merge into one archetypal bag.

No matter where you are in the country, the food will be the same. That's the comfort and that's the terror. But that's not really what McDonald's is trying to sell us.

There is no McDonald anymore, it's just a pleasant name that conjures the pleasant image of Old MacDonald and his harmless farm. What McDonald's *is* is a doorway to another dimension, another world—a different global village with its own citizens: Ronald McDonald and Mayor McCheese, happy families and lovers in love.

But who guards the gates to this other world? Polite teenagers in uniform. What you're buying when you pass under the golden arches is a tiny unit of politeness frozen in time— fast food in friendly bags, bright colors, friendly teens who serve you with a smile, friendly cartoon faces that tell us "we do it all for you." It's all for *me*. It's reassuring. It's a temporary utopia that only lasts as long as your lunch hour.

The signs tell us politely there's a twenty-minute time limit to the booths, the signs in the parking lot give us a half hour. This is the wave of the future. Twenty years from now they won't even serve food, they'll just be politeness centers scattered across the nation, little golden islands in the face of The New Rudeness, islands where you can rest up for the on-slaught of a vicious world.

You can bask in the friendly faces of strangers, but only for a little while. Twenty minutes of affection, that's all you need and that's all you get. Well-dressed men and women will greet you attentively and listen politely for twenty minutes, and then the bad teenagers will come and take you away.

Fast food for the soul. That's McDonald's.

Waiting for a call (L.A.), 10/1/83

National Taste

It's probably official. I saw it on television, in a commercial for one of America's soft drinks. There was a close-up of Coca Cola and a smooth voice-over saying, "If America had an official taste, this would be it." This is an entirely new con-cept in advertising and patriotism. The Eagle is our national emblem; our national taste is Coke. But what about the other senses: What's the national smell? I nominate popcorn, ladies and gentlemen. National touch would be the telephone (as in "Reach Out and Touch"). Americans don't need intimacy, just communication. National sight: rock videos. National sound: annoying electronic pings.

According to the media, America is a healthy young person, white and thirty, laughing on the beach, grabbing the gusto, turning it loose, dancing the night away, working hard, play-ing hard—feeling good about itself. And if this young white person on television feels good, America feels good. As this young white person goes, so goes the nation. It's America in SenSurround and Dolby. We've got a foreign policy, we've got an official taste. We've got senators and lawyers, diet sodas, and wars in small countries. We've got everything we need to quench our thirsts and fill our stomachs.

So why do the soft drinks we drink—no caffeine, no sugar,

no calories—taste like tap water laced with acid bubbles? If our body is becoming America, and America is becoming our body, where's the doctor? What if America gets the flu? Where will America go to the hospital? Does America have medical coverage?

I don't know. I only know that if my body is becoming the body politic, and if my physical senses are linked with the fate of the nation, I'd better start taking better care of myself. No more soda pop. No more malt liquor. I certainly wouldn't recommend malt liquor as the national taste. God no.

On the couch, 9/2/83

Cute

Before I got kicked out of graduate school, I had a job teaching rhetoric. One of my students was a "cute" freshman (she dressed in orange pants suits, with frosted hair and a nose she considered pug, but wasn't). She brought a "War Is Harmful For Children And Other Living Things" poster to class. She brought John Denver records to class, and Harry Chapin. I wasn't as mean to her as I should have been—partly from fear, partly from pity, partly from my need to find out what makes America tick. I did wind up flunking her from my course, but that's not the point.

The point is: when I saw *Annie* (at a date's insistence) I had to hit myself on the head afterward with a small hammer to get that stupid "Tomorrow" song out of my head.

We use up cute fads in this country the way we use up Kleenex, and it's a phenomenon I've never quite understood. Maybe when we buy a little fuzzy stuffed puppy with a tag, "I Wuv Oo," it's a kind of psychic sneeze, a way to rid the collective unconscious of consciousness-blocking mucus. I don't know. I do know there's a constant flow of *cute* in America: troll dolls. Repulsive aliens from outer space. Little two-dimensional dot gobblers. I can understand the fertility rites of certain South American tribes, but the American concept of *cute* is as slippery as Mississippi mud and as elusive as the butterfly of love. The neighborhood shopping mall—the twentieth-century equivalent of the medieval village unit—has entire stores that sell nothing but E.T. dolls, Snoopy-dog dolls, Garfields, Smurfs, Strawberry Shortcakes, and proud unicorns flying over rainbows.

Within our lifetimes—mark our words—plastic surgeons will have the ability to make human beings fuzzy and adorable. With a few strokes of the scalpel we'll all be cute as a bug's ear and cuddly as the day is long.

That day may be drawing near. I received an anonymous Valentine in the mail this year, a card with an idiotic picture of a simpering bear frolicking in a field of daisies and signed simply, "A Secret Admirer." Now I don't know if my secret admirer was being sarcastic, ironic or sincere—who can tell these days?—but I do know I spent a long time comparing the signature to other letters I've received, and frantically examining the postmark for clues to my correspondent's identity before I gave up and threw the damn thing away.

I don't know who you are or what your game is, Secret Admirer, but next Valentine's Day, if you're still around and still admiring, eighty-six the cuddly ursine, give the bum's rush to the cute bear. If you must send me something, send me a postcard of a cowboy riding a giant grasshopper with the caption, "We grow 'em big out here," or send me a "Dig those crazy freeways," or even a postcard of a jackrabbit with antelope horns. You know, send me something I can *use*. Because I white out the message, write my own, then send these cards on to *my* friends. Saves me a bundle at the Hallmark store.

And if you must admire me (something I don't recommend; admiration puts me in a rather sordid and embarrassing position), *sign* your card. Don't worry if I find out your name. I won't remember it anyway, to be quite honest with you. You can go ahead and give me a heartfelt message: "Yours till the end of time," or "I've never loved anybody the way I love you," but *type* it. Forget calligraphy—that kind of fancy hand-writing went out of fashion with the Book of Kells. I don't even mind dot matrix.

But please: don't send me bears. This may not seem like a big deal to you, gentle readers, but this American fascination with bears has always bothered me. It's schizophrenic. The bear is used as a symbol of renewed friendship between Mainland China and the U.S. (in the form of those two pandas who have trouble mating, probably because they've been shuttled from zoo to zoo so much they're too jetlagged to remember which gender is which), *and* we use the bear as a symbol of dread (representing Soviet Russia in Reagan commercials).

Somewhere in the fast in-between of the Panda and murderous Soviet Hulk is the vast cute wasteland of American beardom: the teddy bear, Smokey the Bear, Qantas koalas, Care Bears, jelly bears, Yogi bear, and all those cute greeting cards that say, "I can't *bear* to be without you," or "My love for you is un*bear*able."

I hate to break it to you, America, but a bear is a lumbering half ton of musk, claw and tooth. A bear is smart, unafraid and definitely *not* cute. Why isn't the bear afraid of us? Because we persist in thinking that a bear *is* cute.

I've heard about tourist families who place small children on the backs of bears so they can snap a Polaroid, who hand-feed bears table scraps, who poke them with sticks so they'll stand up on their hind legs and beg.

The consumer market on *cute* is bullish, but *cute* is what puts animals on the endangered-species list in the first place. Wild animals are not cute; they're wild animals, and they belong in the woods, not stuck on your refrigerator with a magnetic piece of fruit.

In line at the P.O., 2/22/85

Vice President

I've never been able to understand exactly what it is that a vice president does. I've seen vice presidents on television, wearing headdresses, eating exotic local foods at social functions, even going to funerals that the President can't attend. The Vice President's job seems to be to display absolute loyalty to the President, making the Vice President (or Veep) the only person in politics with a constituency of one. Not exactly a dynamic job, sort of like (on the surface of things) a Victorian housewife. But for some reason, men have always held this position.

What a President does is obvious. He (or, someday perhaps, she) provides a focus for the nation, a living metaphor of the inner workings of the government. Face it. We watch the government on TV and one person (the President) is a lot easier to look at on that tiny screen than a bunch of Congressmen standing around in a lump. The President *is* the government, a walking talking bundle of jokes, homely metaphors, lively comparisons, tortured syntax, tough talk and a positive attitude.

The Veep is a support system for the President's image. The requirements for Veep have traditionally been strong white teeth, pulsating male rhetoric, a firm handshake, a slight but vigorous nodding of the head whenever the Prez makes a telling point, and hearty male laughter whenever the President tells a joke.

My question is: Can a woman laugh at a man's joke? Is a woman capable of that forced, hearty, throw-back-the-head-and-roar laugh that America seems to love in a politician?

On the bright side, a woman would be great at fireside chats, a woman Veep could keep the First Lady company on those lonely White House nights. And maybe the President will learn how to bake an apple pie, maybe the White House will become a place where the coffee cups are never empty, the doors are never locked, a place where jokes are never laughed at, unless they're funny.

Watching the Dems, July '84

White Lies

White lies help us get through life. We hear white lies at work and play, we tell white lies for pleasure and convenience. We use white lies the way a carpenter uses a hammer:

> Mr. Shoales is on another line. He's away from his desk right now.
>
> Your check's in the mail. Easy to install. Only takes a minute. A child could do it. This won't hurt a bit. Trust me.
>
> Be glad to do it, no problem. Slices, dices, in seconds. Actual mileage may vary. It followed me home, can I keep it? I mailed it a month ago. I'm working late at the office tonight. This is my *real* phone number. I forgot to turn on the machine.
>
> I think of you as a friend. She's just a friend. I need time, time to think, time to be myself.

White lies are an umbrella in the stormy weather of unrelenting truth:

> Beauty is only skin deep. It matches your eyes. She has an interesting personality. You have an interesting face. Your poem is the best poem I've ever read. It was—interesting. I had a wonderful time. It was the best time I've ever had. I'll call you. I love foreign movies. Let's have lunch. We'll do it again sometime.

White lies are Band-Aids on the gaping wound of the morality gap:

> I didn't know you sang so well. You don't act like a Capricorn. Diamonds are a girl's best friend.

Money isn't everything. You're a gem, a jewel, you're irreplaceable. We don't need a contract. If we don't like it we can quit. We can stop any time. We can take it or leave it. Trust me.

White lies give us an excuse to do what we're going to do anyway:

This is just a neighborhood watch. This is just a border patrol. We don't use these weapons, we just have them. This is just national security. These aren't troops, they're advisers. I'm sorry. I didn't mean it.

The end justifies the means. Just little white lies. They help us get through life.

After telling one, 7/22/83

Grenada

Once again President Reagan has proved to be a master of discourse. Posing with the would-be doctors he freed from Grenada, he called opponents to his tiny invasion "smug know-it-alls." How a smug know-it-all *can* know it all in Mr. Reagan's news blackout is news to me, but it's exactly the kind of meaningless rhetorical flourish so dear to the kind of person who writes angry letters to the editor, the kind of person who thinks it was a good idea to keep the press out of Grenada, the kind of person who thinks it was the press who lost the Vietnam war, and not a bunch of airhead generals fighting a determined enemy.

What a foreign policy we have. Our house is on fire in the Mideast, so we go down the Caribbean block, sneak in the back door of another burning house and kick Castro's dog. I can't say if dog kicking will endear us to Latin America, or stop houses from burning, but it seems to make Americans feel better.

Kicking the Cuban dog, kicking the Constitutional dog of a free press, kicking smug know-it-alls when they're down—Mr. Reagan's getting such a kick out of Grenada he doesn't even seem to notice that the very people he rescued represent the smuggest know-it-alls of them all: medical students.

I've never met a humble medical student. I've never met a humble doctor. And what were those medical students doing in Grenada in the first place? Didn't anybody tell them that the med school was in a Marxist country? Maybe they weren't paying attention. Maybe they couldn't get into American medical schools. Whatever the reason, our few good men have brought them home to be better doctors for the experience. And America needs more plastic surgeons.

But the next time one of our houses is burning out of control, instead of airlifting potential osteopaths from a Marxist Club Med, instead of stopping Commies from getting a tan, instead of beating up a nation with roughly the population of Des Moines—the next time, if we're so worried about the safety of Marines and medical students, and the opinions of smug know-it-alls, next time why don't we kill two birds with one policy: Why don't we invade Harvard or Johns Hopkins? Just shut them down. Because kicks keep getting harder to find. We're running out of tiny dogs, and the big dogs, my friends, bite back.

Trying to find the news, November '83

Letters to the Editor

If you ever want to know what America's really thinking, check out the letters to the editor in your local paper. Every opinion you can possibly have is held there by someone. If you want to write your own letter to the editor, all you need are anger, paper, and time to kill. If you're long on paper, but short on time, cheer up: I've written a letter to the editor for you. Take the parts that apply to your political bent and ignore the rest.

* * *

I realize this won't get printed in your so-called newspaper. The (Leftist, Conservative) slant is a disgrace to all (real Americans, taxpayers, our unborn children). Still I must urge everyone to (register to vote, write your Congressman, vote No on Prop 17) or we might not have (another four years, new streetlights, a tomorrow).

As a (taxpayer, life-long Democrat, homeowner) I (view with alarm, am frightened by, am angered by) our (foreign policy, domestic policy, bleeding-heart environmentalists). Are we living in (a welfare state, Nazi Germany, a fool's paradise)?

If we (continue, stop) (support to the arts, defense spending, our present course) how can (our young people, our nation's minorities, the elderly) (smoke in public places, skateboard in safety, survive)? What happened to the Bill of Rights? We're policeman to the world, but we're still the only industrialized nation in the world (without a national health program, with too many handguns).

Therefore I ask Congress to look closely into the (rampant featherbedding, doubledipping, widespread corruption) in the (mass transit system, Pentagon, private sector), which is not only (sexist, frightening, wasteful) but plays into the hands of our enemies. Haven't we learned (that Moscow cannot be trusted, the lesson of Vietnam)?

And if we can't trust our own leaders, is it any wonder it will soon (cost two dollars a gallon, be too late) (for our unborn, to mail a postcard)? This shifty (bleeding heart, big business) trend by (the trilateral commission, pencil pushers in Washington, cabal that killed President Kennedy, New York Liberals, corporate honchos, Nixon, Carter) can only lead to disaster if the (squandering of our precious resources, spiraling military spending, welfare cutbacks) doesn't lead to (jobs for the underprivileged, World War III, a crisis in the Mideast). It's (greed, fuzzy logic) pure and simple.

As a concerned taxpayer, I say it's time to (abandon our so-called allies, call the bluff of our arm-chair patriots, get out of the U.N., annex the Third World). Frankly it (frightens, scares, shocks, sickens, amazes) me. It's a (deplorable, sense-less) tragedy. (Write your Congressman, cancel my subscription) immediately. Haven't we learned anything from history? You probably (will/won't) print this, (and, but) if you print this please don't use my name.

After mailing one, 3/5/84

More Bang for the Buck

Back in the fifties "Our Friend The Atom" was going to usher in a wonderful new world of automated homes, food that stayed fresh forever, cars that ran themselves while Mom and Dad played Yahtzee in the back seat with the kids. The atomic world was warm, comfortable, cozy, and even sexy— the Bikini, after all, was named for a test site.

But then our nation's enemies got atomic. Naturally we started a whisper campaign against their product. This led to fallout shelters, noon sirens, Conelrad, and bigger bombs. We bought the Cold War as we might buy a set of encyclopedias, like good consumers, until we realized that their radioactivity was the same as ours. Red-white-and-blue atomics and Red atomics are the same thing.

Let's call the bomb a car for a minute. We built a car that can only go 5,000 miles per hour. That's quite an achievement, but who's gonna drive the thing, and where? To mix metaphors another way, we've driven the thing into the ground. We got our money's worth. We got more bang for the buck, but maybe the buck better stop here. If Detroit had been running the arms race, they would have taken the bomb off the market in 1962.

Consider the arms race as an ad campaign. The slogan used to be, "If you come in my yard I'll blow up your house." This slogan worked for awhile, it had a nice ring to it, but the basement of our house began to fill up with bombs, and we got a little scared. So we put an aggressive edge to our fear with a new slogan, "Better dead than Red." This wasn't quite as effective, it led to the Cuban missile crisis, and there wasn't much of a future in it, either dead *or* Red. Our present slogan, "We're building these bombs so we will never use them," sounds a lot safer, and it probably is, but setting aside politics for a moment—God forbid that I sound like a liberal—I appeal to your capitalistic common sense. Why are we spending money on something we can't use?

Face it. The fission bomb is an Edsel, a lemon, a dog. Not only a dog, it's a dog with rabies.

After waking, bathed in sweat, 1/28/85

Talking Arms

These days everybody and his dog want to talk with Gromyko. A conversation about bombs with an ancient Russian isn't my idea of a good time, but then again I don't have the highly developed sense of humor that your politician possesses. All I know is we gotta watch out for the Commies. Remember Khrushchev?

We thought Khrushchev wanted to bury us, but he was just nursing a grudge about this whole Disneyland flap. Maybe he just wanted to bury Mickey Mouse. Maybe he was trying out his Donald Duck impression. He couldn't do the voice, so he did the shoe.

And we *were* rude to the guy. If you have a guest in your house you don't scream and call him a lying butcher, even if he is—*especially* if he is. You wait until your guest goes home, then you call him names behind his back. This is called *etiquette*.

If Gromyko wants to go to Disneyland and if the strike's over, I say let him go. Keep it light when you talk to these guys. You gotta work up to the issues—ask Gromyko how his flight was, ask if his limo has a wet bar. Ask him if he thinks the Cubs will win the pennant. Small talk. Crack a couple cold ones and then say, "Oh by the way, what about peace in our time?" You gotta work up to these things, and be careful what you ask for.

Commies are tricky. We told Fidel, "Free your prisoners." He said, "Fine, you take them." So we get political prisoners, Cuban criminals, and a flop Al Pacino movie.

Start small with Gromyko. Ask him for a souvenir—a little bottle of vodka, one of those little surface-to-air missiles. Keep it boring. Do we *want* an interesting government?

My sense of wonder is a bit stunted, I'll admit. I reserve the epic emotions for cosmic events like *Lifestyles of the Rich and Famous* or *Family Feud*. Politics just didn't kick wonder into high gear, and I think that's great.

I want a government as dull and functional as a barbershop. When I go to the barber, I don't want to hear rock music, see bright new-wave colors or hear a debate between "hair stylists." I want to get my hair cut and get out. Same with government.

If I were talking to Gromyko, I'd talk about the weather, the price of meat. I'd keep it as dull as could be. If you want excitement go see *Scarface* or *Red Dawn*.

Politics *is* boring. Voting is boring. Voting is a job. Face it. If you hate your job, you're normal.

And face this: government is as bland as a barbershop, but it's a barbershop with bombs. That's enough excitement for me.

Off the campaign trail, 10/15/84

Journals

They used to be called diaries, and only high-school girls had them. They were little gold-trimmed books kept under tiny lock and key. Some sixteen-year-old girl would curl up in her pink flannels with her tiny gold pen, turn her radio softly to *Top 40* and pen her inmost thoughts, thoughts of dates and quarterbacks. Then, around 1971, schoolteachers found out what these girls were up to in the night, and they got the bright idea to make the girls write these inmost thoughts for *grades*.

Teachers said this helped students organize their thoughts, but I say it's just one more step on that American road where public and private lives are one and the same. Not brave enough to admit that Ralph Waldo Emerson and Walt Whitman were (contrary to popular belief) incredibly dull writers better left to gather dust on the shelf, English teachers tried to pry some "relevance" from these fogeys, to apply these outmoded writers to a modern teenager's life. Not content to let the Beatles be good pop musicians, teachers insisted the Beatles were "poets," thus spoiling the fun for everybody. And, not content to let kids think or not think as they please, they *forced* these kids to have private thoughts, forced kids to view their own lives as if they were television programs, subject to grades, ratings, and cancellation by some jerk who barely squeaked through four years of college with a B.S. in education and a minor in psychology.

And what fruit has come in the '80s of these bad seeds: smug men and women in their late twenties who believe their opinions mean something. Self-satisfied calligraphers. Calligraphy was once the realm of ascetic monks illuminating holy manuscripts, now it's the realm of silly mystics and warmed-over hippies, anybody who can afford a pen. And what is written in this neat hand? Three-by-five index cards on the walls of Laundromats: advertisements for psychic healers, Tai Chi baby-sitters, a nonsmoking single mother who wishes to share her flat with a person who thinks the same way she does.

I sit in the Laundromat, sipping my tepid malt liquor, folding my damp black T-shirts, watching the half-dozen Walkmans nod over hot limp clothes. I watch fine hands dip into journals, in the Laundromats, in the sad cafés. Misspelled words and atrocious grammar, boundless clichés all stroll across the page in shapely lines. I watch them write these journals that will forever remain unread.

Who needs a neat hand in this age of answering machines and Touch-Tone dialing? Who needs a prose style? I know I'll never read another word by Anaïs Nin or Sylvia Plath. These people are losers, no matter what their relevance. I haven't written a letter since 1976. What's the point? I've got postcards. I've got a phone. We're not trying to communicate, but advertise a lifestyle. We only talk to ourselves.

What we buy when we buy is not a product but a set of mental attitudes. There's the instant coffee that's supposed to make you feel like a character in a *New Yorker* story, divorced but still game, walking along a barren New England beach with an Irish setter. There's Paco Rabanne—"What is remembered is up to you." But we don't have any memories of our own. We're secretly disappointed that we have to wash our clothes every week. We're sad that the fog that surrounds us isn't as pearly and thick as the fog in Casablanca, that the boathouse we rented in Connecticut isn't as rustic as the boathouse in *Architectural Digest*. Our memories don't measure up to the vision on the box, and we're left with dusty bottles of foul-smelling aftershave. We're left with the dusty unlocked diaries of our adolescent thoughts. These thoughts used to mean something. Now they're just more empty words in a world that no longer needs them.

In the Laundromat, 8/12/82

School Prayer

The issue of prayer in school gets trotted out every couple of years by dim-witted conservatives who don't have anything important to worry about. I won't presume to speak for God, Whose ears no doubt glow when they hear the heartfelt mutterings of red-cheeked boys and girls. And I can't quarrel with the Norman Rockwell images conjured up by school prayer. I happen to like Norman Rockwell. He painted a world nobody ever lived in, but he was good at painting it.

But let's talk about kids. Let's be honest, folks. Where I grew up, it was hard enough to drum up enthusiasm for the Pledge of Allegiance. Like all public displays of affection, the Pledge of Allegiance always embarrassed me. I'm embarrassed by most group activities—including protest marches, conventions, singalongs, chanting, parades, you name it. And what value does a prepackaged pledge have anyway? Kids didn't write it. The teacher made us stand up and say words that kids wouldn't use in a million years. We didn't know the history of the American flag, we couldn't vote. What does "republic" mean to an eight-year-old kid? An eight-year-old kid understands comic books and skateboards. But "one nation, indivisible"? Forget the strained syntax, what's *indivisible?* Isn't *one* already indivisible? What does mathematics have to do with patriotic duty?

The idea behind school prayer is that kids would have a choice. The kids who don't want to pray won't have to. So what will they do, sit and doodle while the devout bow their heads? Will they get an extra ten minutes of recess? In "one nation, indivisible," this sounds divisive to me. The kids praying will envy the kids playing, and the kids playing will call the praying kids square. The underpaid teachers will have to keep track of this along with everything else. It can only lead to religious persecution, and isn't this what America was founded to escape?

It's a free country, folks, and if you have an atheist eight-year-old—an incongruous thought in itself, like a fish with wheels—that's the price you pay for liberty.

If adults want to nip the godless menace in the bud, that's fine with me, but fight the godless menace in the privacy of your own home. School is for finger painting, multiplication tables, and making friends. Pray at home, pray in church. But fight the good fight on your own time; leave the kids out of it. The only thing they'll pray for anyway is better grades and a longer recess. Believe me, I've been there.

Not in church, 3/15/84

Teachers in Space

I'm with you, Mr. President. First there was the joke about blowing up Russia; that's great, that's part of the famous Republican sense of humor, the envy of the free world, the kind of humor that made Joan Rivers a role model for women everywhere. Then there was the famous cricket affair, a potential crisis, resolved I assume by the Secret Service, who wrestled the hapless insect to the ground and kept those tiny sleep-destroying legs from rubbing together. That's great too. That's our tax dollars at work. Now Mr. Reagan wants to send a teacher into space. A teacher-in-space program! How whimsical can you get?

When I was in fifth grade I would have loved it if Miss Norgaard had cruised a couple of times around the earth. The farther away she was from me, the better off we both were. The idea, though, of poor Miss Norgaard in a space suit seems rather incongruous. She *never* wore slacks, and all her dresses looked like upholstery material. Is that the look NASA is shooting for? And here's what I *really* want to know: Is sending a teacher into space a punishment or a reward?

There's been a mixed attitude toward the teaching profession in this country ever since Abraham Lincoln totted up figures on a coal shovel, then walked 400 miles barefoot in a blizzard, or hailstorm, or whatever the hell it was, just to return a book. Republicans love stories like that. They'd love it if everybody taught themselves and then made a million bucks telling others how to do it. The trouble with America is that teachers aren't millionaires. But I really don't see how shooting them into space will shoot them into another tax bracket, and it seems a pretty expensive way to get rid of a bad teacher.

Now, I know this is supposed to be a learning experience. Miss Norgaard will go around the globe a couple of times, have a mystical experience, and return to earth a better teacher. She will transmit her enthusiasm to apple-cheeked eager youngsters, and they in turn will grow up to be cops, astronauts, and CEO's for offshore corporations.

But wouldn't it be easier to put astronauts in the classroom? Give Buzz Aldrin a teaching certificate and turn him loose. Or, send *all* the teachers into space. Even better, send all the kids into space. Build a high school out there—school colors black and white. Use the space shuttle as a school bus, and build a huge airtight log-cabin schoolhouse in the sky, grades K through 12. They'll read from McGuffey's Reader, and pray, of course. Recess will be the only problem, unless kids can learn how to play Red Rover in a vacuum.

Can the taxpayer afford teeny space suits for the tots? Will the space suits be *cool* enough for the style-conscious teen of tomorrow? But these questions are mere quibbles. I'm with you, Mr. President. I just wish I was a kid again to appreciate the glorious vacuum you have painted so grandly. I wish I was a kid so I could say, "Beam me up Miss Norgaard! I'm ready to learn!"

Watching the skies, 9/1/84

Buzzwords

Politicians look like a fun bunch at conventions. The spectacle of grown men and women blowing horns, playing with donkeys and elephants—it sort of erases the line between a political party and a just-plain party. It appeals to the child in a politician, I guess. And we have enough childish politicians, which makes me wonder: Is the democratic process a healthy thing to show America's young?

When I was a kid, politics scared the wits out of me. Certain insidious phrases crept into my vocabulary, words like "dark horse," "hat in the ring," "lame duck," "cold war," "iron curtain." What's a kid today supposed to think when the President is accused of practicing voodoo economics? A kid knows what voodoo is. It turns people into zombies on *Creature Features*. The image of President Reagan dancing around the Oval Office balancing the budget on his nose as he sacrifices a chicken to the gods of deficit spending will probably not inspire today's young person to become an accountant. But television won't show us executive branch *obeah*. No, they wouldn't show us the iron curtain when I was a kid either.

Even today, in 1984, when a Republican spokesman said the President needed wiggle room on the platform for a tax increase, I found myself thinking, "Gee, a wiggle room. That sounds like a fun place to go." And if the Republican platform can't even provide a lousy wiggle room for a President of the United States, how can we pretend to our children this is a just and fair world?

One man's mixed metaphor is another man's poison, and grown-up slogans are the essence of preteen mythology. There's no solution. You just have to tell your kids that the world of politics and money is a complicated world. When the going gets tough, the tough get audited. Explain it as best you can, but if your kids wander away during your explanation, don't worry about it too much. You'll probably find them downstairs in the wiggle room, playing dark horsey with the lame duck.

Watching the Reps, August '84

BUSINESS AND ECONOMY

Sugar

I came across a term the other day in my favorite publication (no, not *Grit*, though that's a pretty good rag). I'm speaking of the *National Enquirer*, which isn't a newspaper so much as the perfect way to kill that half hour you spend between putting your food on the supermarket conveyor belt and bouncing the check to the surly teenager at the register. The term I read was "holiday fat," which struck me as the most American concept ever. Holiday fat. Seasonal body weight. Holiday fat is a problem, according to the *National Enquirer* and of course they suggest in their breathless way many harebrained means to get rid of it.

Our nation's attitude toward bodies is a strange one. On the one hand we're encouraged to overeat on holidays, but on the other we're discouraged from gaining weight. Our corporations get Americans hooked on sweets and then scare us about eating sweets. We drank quarts of coffee and then were told caffeine is bad for us. So now we have coffee that isn't coffee, Coke that isn't Coke, margarine that isn't butter, sugar that isn't sugar, NutraSweet that isn't saccharine. . . . When we nail down the knack of gene splicing, we'll have a person that isn't a person: People Lite.

The whole sugar controversy is linked directly to the arms race. We want to show off how prosperous we are—that is, we want the world to see we're fat and sassy, but we want to be physically fit at the same time, so we won't be pushovers for lean and hungry barbarians from the East. This schizophrenic attitude goes on and on. Remember: Snickers are the official snack food of the '84 Olympics. Sure. Decathlon runners snarf down those Snickers by the truckload.

And if they don't, they should. We have to remember, sugarwise, that the economy of many a third-world country is directly dependent on little children's desire for Sugar Whackies on Saturday mornings. Nobody has ever explored the economic relationship between Saturday morning cartoons and the fate of sugar-producing third-world countries. When Mighty Mouse went into reruns, Cuba collapsed. Is this a coincidence? If we stop eating sugar, who's going to support these third-world countries? I'll tell you who. Lean and hungry barbarians from the East.

I think there's probably a relationship between the rise of Metrecal and the rise of Castro. Sure, sugar is empty calories, but I think we have a patriotic duty to consume as much of it as we can. It's a cavity-causing form of charity, but charity *should* hurt. And as our waistline expands, so will the economy of our neighbors to the south. We're in Fat City, my friends, don't let the specter of thinness rear its ugly head. The next time some third-world country collapses, because the sugar market has gone to the dogs, remember what I said. And eat a candy bar. Put teeth in the Monroe Doctrine. Your teeth.

Watching Scoobie Do, *2/9/84*

The Agony of Self-Employment

On the top of my 1040 it says "Ian Middle Initial Shoales," Occupation, Social Critic. On the top of my head I wear a felt snap-brim Bogart hat. When I fill out my 1040, my E form, my SE form, my 4625 Section 178; when I fill out Part II Schedule C deductions; when I run down the list of ways to whittle down the income, where is the category called "Hats"? Don't look it up, hipsters and hippettes. Take it from me, it's not there.

The IRS doesn't understand that the whole *film noir* iconography represented by my hat contributes to my self-image, and my self-image is important to my ego, and my ego drives me to be a social critic, and Social Critic is the occupation that makes me money to give to the IRS in the first place. So why won't they let me deduct the hat?

I admit it, I used to be broke and obnoxious in the counter culture, but now I'm obnoxious in the over-the-counter culture. I'm trying to make money now, trying to render unto Caesar that which is the Taxman's. But give me a break, IRS. Let me deduct the hat.

I accept that you wouldn't let me deduct $150,000 worth of entertainment expenses last year. I accept that you don't believe I saw 8,000 movies last year. I don't keep receipts. Most of the movies and concerts I see, I'm lucky to escape with my life, much less a receipt. I accept that you wouldn't let me depreciate my parents' house. After all, I haven't lived there since 1968, but let me deduct the hat. Let me wear it with pride.

I want to feel like I've put something over on someone, just like the corporate boys. And the next time I hobnob with waitresses, cabbies, grannies, and baby-sitters, the people who (according to *Time)* are bringing the IRS to its knees by not reporting their petty cash—the next time I have a cup of joe at 3 A.M. with my hat tilted back, and my Bic busy scribbling biting social commentary, I'll remember you, IRS, and be kind. Now I've mentioned the hat. It's the subject of this essay. I bought it for my occupation. I've got the receipt. I am *going* to deduct the hat. The next time I get audited I'll have something nice to wear.

At the mailbox, 4/14/82

Temp Work

Along the way to my present success I've had to work for a living, usually at "temp work," as it's called in professional circles. I have moved furniture, filed, typed, answered phones, and I probably have the world's record for getting fired. This is because I'd show up at work unshaven, wearing sunglasses and not wearing socks. I figured, "I'm not an executive, who's gonna care?" Well, after my third temp job in a week, I finally took Mom's long-distance advice, got a beige seersucker three-piece for five bucks at Goodwill. It fit me like a glove, and I wore it to my next temp job. But when the permanent employees saw me approach the water cooler, they all scattered. Nobody would come near me. Finally a little bald guy worked up the courage to ask me who I was. He had me pegged as some corporate honcho checking up on worker efficiency, I guess, because when I told him I was a temp worker, a look of relief passed over his face. Then he replaced that look with one of utter disregard. By noon, all employee fear of me had vanished. So the next day my suit vanished to be replaced by blue jeans, and the next day my job vanished to be replaced by poverty.

But if you're an artist of any kind, it means you're going to *have* to get the kind of job you get till you get to do what you want to do. So let me give you some advice about the temp-worker scene.

Never drink beer at your desk. Supervisors don't like it.

Permanent employees probably won't appreciate your Joe Cocker impression.

If you're moving furniture, don't move a desk if somebody's sitting at it.

Never call corporate executives by their first name, or ask them if they want to play a couple of holes on Saturday.

Don't try to find Pac Man on the personal computer unless you're invited by your supervisor.

Never ask the supervisor for a date.

If you're answering the company phone, say "Hello," not "Yeah, what do ya want?"

I know temp work can get dull, but never rearrange the filing system without permission.

Don't rewrite business letters in blank verse.

If you're supposed to show up at work on Tuesday don't come in on Wednesday.

I know this is basic stuff, but don't draw faces with white-out on the desk; don't make jewelry out of the paper clips; don't compose melodies on the Touch-Tone phone; don't ask to borrow the Selectric overnight—remember always, you're just a ghost in the working world.

Somebody will eventually publish the 1,500-page rock-and-roll novel gathering dust in your sock drawer. Your ship will come in, and then you'll have temps of your own. And they better not call you by your first name.

Not rich, 1/15/84

Get Rich Quick

I suppose it's too late now to expect my life to turn into a Horatio Alger novel. After all, I was never an orphan boy, I was probably never a boy, never had a newsstand—I never even had a paper route. But still, a boy can dream can't he? I never had the rags, but there's still the riches. There must be some John Beresford Tipton, some Howard Hughes at least, some Michael Anthony, some trillionaire's emissary who admires my spunk, who admires my gumption enough to fork over a seven-figure check. All right. It won't happen and I guess I'm glad about it. That much money would interfere with what's left of my spiritual nature.

And money doesn't buy happiness, and happiness sure doesn't buy money. Look at Edie Sedgwick, look at the children of movie stars, look at movie stars. Rich people aren't happy, goes the myth, just rich. Even Daddy Warbucks needed his Annie.

I don't have the big bucks and I ain't got Annie either, but I do all right as a social commentator. In my spare time, though, like everyone else, I think of get-rich-quick schemes. Now that fame and fortune are dropping on me like fleas on a dog, I thought I'd part with a few of my money-making ideas. Do with them what you will.

Pornographic playing cards and postcards with jackalopes. I don't know who buys these things, but every truck stop in the country sells them, there must be a market for them. Make coffins for dead pet rocks. I realize the idea's a little dated, but keep the principle. Wait until Cabbage Patch dolls go out of style and make cute little coffins for them. If you've got a tape recorder go into the answering-machine business—make prepackaged messages and peddle 'em to people too busy to make their own. Put commercials on postage stamps. Put commercials on money.

What about generic condos? The building is all white and labeled "condo." The microwave is labeled "microwave," the TV is labeled "TV." Everything is white and reasonably priced. Real-estate developers, take note.

Finally my tour de force: my movie. *Vengie*. *Vengie* is the story of a cute little terrier mutt that a family tries to take to the vet. Vengie escapes and spends the rest of the movie terrifying the family in cute ways. *Cujo* sort of stole my thunder with this idea, but giving Cujo rabies was a cheat. Dogs don't need a disease to be ill-tempered. No more than humans. I'm ill-tempered all the time, but still sort of lovable, or at least not beneath contempt.

When *Vengie* is released, we'll put out the calendar: "Scary Puppies '85," showing cuddly little spaniel pups snarling at the camera. And dolls. How about an Ian Shoales doll? It'll make a million. Pins optional. The Ian Shoales dream house. Ian Shoales and Barbie. Heh heh. It boggles the mind.

Still not rich, 2/9/84

CRIME

Cute Names for Killers

I don't believe in taping TV shows. If God had meant me to
remember old TV shows, He would have given me a photo-
graphic memory. But I wish I had a tape of the old *Tomorrow*
show in which Tom Snyder interviewed Charles Manson. As
revelations go, there weren't many, but it was still quite a
spectacle, if you like bear-baiting, and the bear is a white-
trash acid head with more brains than the baiter. In America,
we'll put a beast in the cage of public scrutiny and poke it
with sticks. We call this a public service. We call this psychology.

One of the dearest liberal beliefs in this country is that
understanding a problem and solving it are the same thing.
And mad-dog killers have problems like everybody else. I
guess we want to know what makes them tick. And I guess
they're willing to tell us.

The killer usually has a nickname—Hillside Strangler,
Zodiac Killer, Jack the Ripper, Green River Slayer, Son of
Sam. Even the killer of the universe has a cute nickname—
the Quark. A killer has a nickname, or no name at all.

But does a nickname really help us understand a killer?
Once a killer is located on the grid of pathology—a paranoid
schizophrenic, a disappointed office seeker, a man in love
with Jodie Foster—once the killer is pinned to the map of
medical opinion like a moth, is the killer rendered harmless?
No. The only thing that happens is the nameless killer has a
name, and once the beast has a name, we hope that it, like a
dog, will come at our command.

But the beast usually chooses these names himself to transform himself into something he is not: not a dog, but a man

who matters, a man who alters the course of events by acts of destruction. A random killing isn't a crime of passion, but an act of criticism. Life is a book to these monsters, and they rip out human lives like pages from a novel they wish they could have written.

Cold-blooded is as close to a description as we'll get. A random killing is the dark side of a miracle, a lightning bolt of human nature, an accident of passion and missed opportunities. A killer caught in this scheme of things is a killer rewarded; a killer found guilty is a killer made a movie star, a nickname screaming from the headlines. Then America moves on to the next sensation, a few citizens fewer, with a few more unsolved disappearances, a few more cute names for killers in our heads, more useless information only good for Trivial Pursuit, and a few more nagging questions:

What happened to Hallowe'en? What happened to the unlocked door? Why must we teach children to run from the smile of a stranger? Now the sweet world has a bitter core—a razor in the chocolate, a knife behind an open grin, an invitation from a darkened car. Farewell, Hershey's Kisses. The kiss is poison. Only adults eat chocolate now—Swedish chocolates, exclusive chocolates, chocolates with tight security.

A tiny minority of insane people has altered America's social history. This is a world with mean tricks and no treats now, a world where all pleasures contain their own pain, all crimes their own punishment, and punishment is its own reward. It's a world where the bogeymen are real.

Waiting for kids, 10/31/84

Gun Control

I believe you only need a gun for two things: to kill rattlesnakes and stop cattle stampedes. If you live in the city you need a telephone, not a gun. If you're robbed, wait till the thief goes away, then call the police. There's no messy moral issue, no blood on the floor, just a brisk touch of the Touch-Tone, and it's out of your hands. And the telephone's cheaper than a gun. Also consider the lawsuits and legal fees incurred by killing an intruder in today's society. And a thief, after all, is just trying to make a buck like anybody else. Call the cops. Cops may be rude, they may be slow, but they know how to use a gun, and that's a lot more than you can say about most gun owners. Gun owners make a habit of keeping a gun in a night table by the bed, where it's found by curious youngsters, or used by couples to kill each other in arguments about who loves each other the most. Sometimes gun owners keep handguns locked in a safe place, where they don't do much good against a burglar, and are probably in fact stolen by burglars while the gun owner sleeps the well-protected sleep. Then these guns find their way into the hands of professional criminals who either kill each other in gambling arguments or in what our journalists cutely call "gangland" slayings. It's obvious that we don't need gun control; all our gun owners are killing each other off.

Movies and television somehow get blamed for the morality of their viewers. Blaming a movie like *Deer Hunter* for the gullibility of its audience is like blaming the Beatles for Charles Manson or Jodie Foster for John Hinckley. There's no way we can stop psychopaths from owning a television set, or from making a movie, for that matter. Or from owning a gun. I think this is healthy. A nation on a hair trigger is a well-protected nation. A well-protected nation doesn't need Valium, just more emergency rooms. And a nation without people doesn't need protection at all.

In ancient Celtic mythology satire was used as a weapon—words actually had the power to kill. Today's libel laws have made that impossible, of course, but my main weapon will continue to be pure unapologetic unconstructive sarcasm. Sarcasm doesn't really change anything, or hurt anybody for that matter, but it sure makes *me* feel better.

On the couch, 3/5/84

Libel

When I was in high school the principal threatened me with a libel suit. He wouldn't relax the dress code, so I called him a fascist in the high-school paper. I don't know why he got so upset. When I called my parents fascists all they did was kick me out of the house.

I asked the senior-class president and year-book editor, a blond jerk with unnaturally white teeth—I think he'd had them capped in grade school—to defend me in court. I figured he was destined for a career in law and mine would be a landmark case. He was mildly interested until his father told him he'd kick *him* out of the house if he had anything more to do with me. It was just as well. There just wasn't room for two to sleep in my '63 VW—and besides, the VW would have been the legal fee.

It all worked out for the best, however. The principal dropped the suit, I got a haircut, and my folks let me come home, but it just goes to show you, the life of a gadfly on the body politic isn't all beer and skittles. Sticks and stones might break the bones, but it's the printed word that brings in the lawyers.

Which makes me wonder: what is honor in the modern world? When you say "That insults me," does it really mean, "My lawyers think I have a good case"? Does prestige come with a legal retainer? Can a blush be used as evidence? Is a legal staff a prerequisite to a damaged reputation?

It seems to me a damaged reputation is purely a rich man's burden, once avenged with duels. Now, I enjoy the image of General Westmoreland and the *Sixty Minutes* gang taking measured paces with pistols at dawn, but those dueling days are gone, and the days when the word had cutting power are gone too.

Take the bizarre case of Falwell versus Flynt. God knows, I don't hold Reverend Falwell as a role model (though he certainly has a reputation to uphold), but how can anything said by Mr. Flynt possibly affect that reputation? How seriously can you take *Hustler*'s opinion on anything? Take the *National Enquirer*. Suing them is like calling a spade a spade. You're not fooling anybody or changing anything, you're only translating your own embarrassment into a court settlement, and it's lawyers who get the blood from the stone of libel suits.

We have a superstitious fear of the printed word, of its power to harm us, so we draw a magic circle of legal briefs around it. Or we raise a mountain of red tape to stop the avalanche of information; ratings systems and the FCC tell us who can see what; books are burned, banned, ignored by critics, albums smashed, tapes erased, lawsuits filed. Psychologists and bureaucrats bury simple words in a mountain of jargon, a mountain of lies and truth, information and disinformation.

And what is information but something to be used by those who have it against those who don't? The networks give it out to win a ratings battle; the CIA keeps it in the national interest; the KGB distorts it in the national interest; advertisers select it so we will buy their products; we collect it to spread gossip about our friends; we smear it on our enemies; we use it as blackmail; we stick it to those we hate; for every Shakespeare play there's an enemies list. One of the reasons Dante wrote the *Inferno* was to put his enemies in the fires of Hell. That's probably the main reason I write. Vengeance. Envy. Money.

All of this just goes to show I'm glad I'm not in high school anymore. I'm too old, for one thing; and I don't have a lawyer, for another. And it shows that those who say the pen is mightier than the sword are liars. Ask yourself: would you rather be called nasty names in the newspaper or pierced with a sharp instrument? I say, "No contest." I don't care what you call me, I've called myself worse. Compared to the real problems of the world, humiliation is a minor and temporary inconvenience. Only now, in these self-indulgent times, is personal embarrassment elevated to tragedy. That's my opinion. If you don't like it, sue me.

Reading an old yearbook, 12/10/84

FASHION

The Body

It used to be easy to dress casually. Ward wore a cardigan when he relaxed, and June wore a frock, even in the kitchen. Mr. Rogers is still a cardigan holdover, but the line between casual and sophisticated has somehow been erased. America used to adore a swell, but the only men who wear tuxedoes these days are either British spies, or waiters, or some guy hanging around to make Joan Collins look good.

This holds true for women too. Grace Kelly has been replaced by Jennifer Beals, and Diane Keaton has been replaced by Boy George. You can buy your clothes pretorn *à la Flashdance;* you can dress for success; you can dress to please the opposite sex, to please the same sex, to dress *like* the opposite sex—nobody cares anymore.

The playboy philosophy is on the wane, the barber pole has been replaced by the hair stylist's neon, and jogging clothes can be worn into the fanciest restaurant without putting the slightest dent in a waiter's sneer. Now that designer clothes come off the assembly line, high fashion is within reach of most pocketbooks, but beauty today is more than skin deep, and it's more than beauty. Personal hygiene in the '80s has been elevated into high art.

Take hair. Hair used to be just hair. You could tame it into submission with little dabs of goo and a comb. But today hair has to bounce; it has to fluff; it has to have a life of its own; it has to look like it wants to escape from the head altogether. Look at Tina Turner. Look at David Lee Roth.

Hair can't be hair anymore. Disguising hair is achieved by a bizarre process called *feathering*. Feathering demands special scissors, combs, brushes, and a blow dryer—a small torture device that blows scalding air streams at your damp hair. Towels are outmoded, my friends, and shampoo gets its own aisle in the supermarket.

You can buy shampoo that is "self-regulating," whatever that means. There are shampoos for dry, oily, or normal hair. Shampoo with lemon, wheat germ, coconuts, apples, shampoo you can almost eat. Shampoo is more than just soap. It has *secret ingredients*. It's designed to *transform* your hair, the way alchemy turns lead into gold. We turn hair into something else by eliminating all the things that make hair hair. Like dandruff, for example.

Dandruff today is more than just a mild inconvenience; it is an embarrassment so total it can kill you. Even the *suggestion* of dandruff can be socially lethal, as in, "She's scratching her head. That could be dandruff." Dandruff today is a virus, a mysterious toxic presence in the body. To get at the source of dread-dandruff leakage, shampoo goes deep, all the way to the roots, as deep as a razor blade, to enter all the secret places of the body where dandruff dwells, to root out and destroy dandruff, bad breath, sweat, dirt, grease—everything, in short, that makes a body a body.

This cosmetic strip mining is designed to make our hair the hair of angels, to make a body that's truly worthy of the clothes we buy. And now we have perfect bodies in perfect clothes, a body without lust and without desire, content with itself, content in self-admiration.

We can admire these new bodies anywhere. Our tables are so clean we can see ourselves in them. Our glasses are so clean we can see ourselves in them. Everything in the house is a mirror. There's no reason to go outside. We've got our clothes, we've got our perfect bodies. And that's America in a nutshell—all dressed up and no place to go.

In a strange bathroom, 7/2/84

STYLE

Sophistication

There are some among us who yearn for the sophistication of an earlier age—William Powell and Myrna Loy knocking back highballs high over art-deco Manhattan. Naturally that ultrasophistication went hand in hand with severe alcohol abuse. Hard drinking was once thought charming, a mark of high intelligence and style. Nobody opposed the sophistication of drinking but Eliot Ness and Carrie Nation.

If you didn't drink in those days, you were some kind of sentimental sap—a poor mother in rags singing "Daddy Come Home" outside the saloon on a Friday night. But the main concept, unique to the time, was to drink vast quantities of alcohol and not show it. This was called "holding your liquor." Hemingway, Hammett and Fitzgerald were supposed to drink with the left hand, knock out elegant prose with the right, and spend their spare time arm wrestling and sneering at one another's prose style. Drinking was heroic. The hangover was a badge of courage.

Alcohol is unhip now, unless it's white wine and light beer. Grab the gusto, but don't get drunk. Things are different, but not that different. For all our talk of alcoholism as a disease, it's still considered a character flaw at worst and sort of cute, like Dudley Moore in *Arthur*. And you don't see sophisticated society dames in their seal furs singing "Daddy Come Home" to their three-martini-lunch stockbroker husbands. No, today we have the discreet clinics that can afford to advertise on television, help that is just a phone call away. Oh sure, they say the phone call is hard to make, but all you really need is a major credit card, and the staff of experts will leap into that alcohol problem, solve it, and then run the ten miles home.

Today the hip thing to do is get high on your body. Running huge distances is supposed to provide a feeling of euphoria and elation. There are entire magazines devoted to running, which the runner pores over for types of shoes, in the same way a sophisticate sniffs through a wine list. Only in rich America can severely monklike behavior turn into self-indulgence.

If drinking historically was considered the mark of a great soul and good conversation—ghost stories over brandy, Cole Porter over cocktails, romance over fine wine—now non-drinking is transformed into a mark of virtue. We used to drink and not act drunk, now we try to get drunk by not drinking.

The function of exercise used to be to make the body fit for battles and chores. Now we get fit to get high. And as far as drinking problems go, if credit cards and Touch-Tone phones are necessary adjuncts to will power, I'd say we're still a nation of drunks and over-the-hill jocks. Our running shoes are a pathetic badge of mortality. You can't outrun the grim reaper, folks, or drink him under the table either.

Not drinking or running, 5/4/84

Things I Didn't Do This Summer

Certain magazines and columnists make what they like to call a Summer Reading List. Not only are you supposed to broil yourself raw on the beach, you're supposed to give yourself a headache trying to wade through the dry prose of a book you couldn't even drag yourself through in college when your brain was young. It's never a small book like *Jonathan Livingston Seagull*, which at least would be over quickly, it's always a large dusty book like *War and Peace, Don Quixote*, or the five-volume annotated biography of Franz Kafka. Let me clue you, if the book is thicker than my wrist I won't read it, and I didn't.

And I didn't try to figure out who Harold Robbins was *really* writing about and I didn't count the number of times the pronoun *I* was used in the self-serving autobiography of some faded Hollywood star. I didn't gaze with a fixed grin on the latest picture book about cats. I didn't read the 5,000-page science-fiction trilogy set in an alternative universe where cardboard characters and tortured prose are the norm. I didn't work out a success program *or* my body. I didn't get a tan. I didn't see a 3-D movie. Three-D is the Edsel of special effects. It died once, let it die again. I didn't catch up on any fads: no wind-surfing, Frisbee, or softball. I didn't go to camp. I didn't mow the lawn. I didn't climb a mountain or solve a whodunit. Vacation ideas are ideas from hell, and I wouldn't touch them if you paid me, and certainly not in my free time.

Why is it that vacation time is always the time you're supposed to do the things you wouldn't be caught dead doing? Like painting the house or washing the car, or catching up on your reading, or checking out the new fads? Pet rocks, hula hoops, the twist, disco, money markets, videoscreens the size of a basketball court, holograms—these things died for a reason.

If you must have the illusion of doing something during your leisure hours, do like I do. Enter contests and lotteries. Write a letter to Ann Landers (she's easier to fool than you think). Subscribe to a Jehovah's Witnesses magazine. (It only costs a buck for a year; the arguments against evolution aren't convincing, but the illustrations of middle-class families enjoying Paradise after the Last Judgment are all first-rate.) If you must feel useful think of a gimmick that will make you a million dollars. Think of Cinerama and Smell-O-Vision. Think of Woody Allen. To give *Zelig* a look of authenticity, he dragged the footage through the dirt. Think of it, millions of Americans lining up to see a movie that was dragged through dirt. I'm going to rush out and see it myself, as soon as I get some free time.

Not on the beach, 9/19/84

Whither Hayley Mills?

A while back I was watching Saturday morning cartoons when a McDonald's commercial came on. Mayor McCheese was talking in a cute voice to what looked like a big purple rug with legs. My jaw dropped and I found myself screaming at the television, "What the hell is that thing?" I'm sure many American kids are screaming that same question. When we turn on the tube we're asked to accept some pretty bizarre characters and relationships. A talking car? A bionic man? A dog who hunts ghosts? You didn't have to make these great leaps of faith when I was a kid. Characters were obvious. You were in love with either Hayley Mills or Annette Funicello.

Now, I'm a Hayley man from way back. I've still got my Davy Crockett coonskin cap, and let me tell you, if they ever revive the Mickey Mouse Club and they need a replacement for Jimmy, I might be persuaded to set aside my bad attitude long enough to introduce Spin and Marty one more time. Why not? I'm a sap like everybody else. I've been to Disneyland fifteen times. When you pass through the gates, you enter a world where pirates are cute, gophers can sing, and President Lincoln can actually stand up and talk at the same time. It's always 1955, and the older I get the more I appreciate that. If the underpaid teenagers who pick up the litter seem a little bored and the friendly smiles sometimes seem a little fixed, well, even paradise has a price. And the price for paradise gets higher all the time.

One of our great grotesque rumors is the rumor that Walt Disney had himself fast-frozen, cryogenically stopped in time, so he'll be ready to thaw in the twenty-first century, when they will have the cure for everything. Then Uncle Walt will come back to life, like a vampire or a Rip Van Winkle, to create more miracles in a future better prepared to deal with them.

These are confusing times, and the lines around our lives are often drawn by a shaky hand. Disney's hand was firm, and the world he drew is clear. Like the Playboy Empire, Disneyland is a kingdom based on one man's vision. The death of Walt Disney is like the death of God.

Without Uncle Walt behind the scenes we can't accept Disney World, or Epcot Center. We can't make the mental leaps demanded by amusement parks. We sit in the moving car, taped voices singing in our ears, watching the artificial world go by. It's like being inside a video game. When we ride that ride we're expressing a human desire to disappear or be manipulated by God, to be coin-operated by a benign and wise game player.

But without Walt we can't believe in the artificial world, the rides, the video games, the space movies. It's hard to vanish inside them. Sure, we're amazed that the funny gopher can sing, but it's the same amazement we occasionally feel when we turn on a light. It's a miracle, but one you get used to. And a light bulb at least gives us light. A talking bear just gives us a bizarre image that only lasts as long as the ride—then we join the throng of tourists once again. If talking bears aren't a figment of Walt Disney's imagination, then they're just more random corporate images unconnected to anything.

We only need these cute images to justify our technology. Going to the moon isn't enough. Computers and heat-seeking missiles aren't enough. The electronics aren't real to America until a billion preteenagers have dropped their quarters into Donkey Kong.

It's empty fun. The old cartoons gave us Bugs and Fudd and Mickey and Donald in an awesome mythological world of cruelty and reincarnation. Even if Bugs dropped an A-bomb on Fudd, he'd come back together for the chase. It's a perfect parallel to certain versions of the Isis-Osiris myth. But so what?

The amusement park without an uncle is a spectacle that doesn't want us. It's predigested food. Pac Man wilts, comes back, devours, and is devoured. As long as we've got quarters, television, or the price of admission, these creatures will live, and the cold spectacle will continue.

But listen, maybe Walt Disney will come back. And until that time, if Hayley Mills is still available, somebody tell her I'm available too. I'll wait for her at the Matterhorn, she'll recognize me right away. I'll be the pale skinny guy in the threadbare coonskin cap.

In line for Space Mountain, *2/20/85*

Comedy

There are two kinds of comedy: sophomoric and sophisticated. In sophomoric comedy, two fraternity guys swap one-liners about breast sizes and then pour beer on each other's head. In sophisticated comedy two guys in tuxedoes swap one-liners about the theater and then pour champagne on each other's head. It's all a question of environment. This is the basic dichotomy Bergson didn't see when he wrote his famous essay on the mechanics of laughter.

Alright, I've never read that essay, but I know we don't laugh at a joke because it's funny, we laugh at a joke because that's what we're supposed to do. Look at the past—Chaplin, Keaton, the anarchy of the Marx Brothers, so much admired by the psychotic French aesthetes of the '30s. Then we moved into chimpanzee jokes, funny dogs, Doris Day, bedroom humor, Little Willy jokes, Mommy Mommy jokes; finally we moved into cartoons of outhouses and desert islands. We had jokes about hunters and traveling salesmen. We saw cartoons of men reeling down the street at 3 A.M. with little *x*'s over their eyes, spilling their martinis when their battle-ax wives hit them over the heads with rolling pins. And then came the '60s. Nothing was funny in the '60s. We thought *Laugh-In* was funny in the '60s.

Then the '70s brought a Comedy Renaissance: anorexic women and hyperactive men; silly pointless jokes on Saturday Night by smug leering emotional basket cases whose only claim to a sense of humor was their audacity, boldness, and willingness to see how much they could sneak by the censors without getting thrown into FCC Prison. I'm sorry, gentle reader, but humor is a one-way ticket to Palookaville. You want to make money, get into cocaine dealing.

I saw a "performance piece" the other night. We sat in a warehouse listening to tapes of laundromats and trucks, as seven naked women on bicycles wheeled slowly around the performance space.

Halfway through the piece, one of the twelve people in the audience began howling with laughter and ran out of the space, his laughter echoing behind him. I don't know if the laughter was part of the artist's concept, or whether it was nervous laughter of some poor sap who can't get behind the new aesthetics, but I do know this: some people laugh at conceptual art, some people laugh at jokes, some people laugh at car accidents. Me, I haven't laughed since 1972. Laughter takes too much time.

Not laughing, 12/21/81

How I Spent the Holidays

I spent the holidays trying to visit a girlfriend who didn't want to see me. I could understand that. I wouldn't want to see me either, but my holiday plans went out the window in her large Midwestern town, and instead of spending time in her nice warm apartment, I spent a week in a cheap motel in the dead of winter. The motel had everything you need in a cheap motel room: HBO and a hideous abstract painting bolted to the wall. Every cheap motel room in the country has a hideous abstract painting bolted to the wall. Why is it bolted to the wall? Is the motel afraid I will steal the painting? I don't want the damn painting, I just want to stuff it under the bed until checkout. I thought abstract expressionism was another fad like the hula hoop, so why do these things keep showing up on bank and motel-room walls? Who makes these things? Who buys them?

All you can do is throw a sheet over these paintings, which helped me to concentrate on HBO showing Steve Martin in *Pennies from Heaven*. What's a great movie like that doing on cable? If *Pennies from Heaven* had been a foreign movie it would have made a million bucks. It makes me furious that a genuinely funny man like Steve Martin is falling by the public wayside just because he's too popular. Too many frat guys put arrows through their heads, too many fat teenage boys said, "I am a wild and crazy guy." We heard a thousand Excu-u-u-use me's, but only ten of them were Steve Martin's. There are people who were sick of Steve Martin before they'd even seen him. Is that his fault?

Why are his movies on cable and a movie like *Scarface* still in the theaters? All right, I haven't seen *Scarface*, but why should that stop me from having an opinion on it? Everybody else does. I read a column by George Will saying that *Scarface* should have been rated "X" because parents were taking their children to see it. So what? Why should the motion-picture industry be responsible for our morality?

Dad says to Mom, "*Scarface* is in town."

"What's it about?"

"Human scum who kill each other over cocaine deals."

"Sounds great! Let's take the kids!"

There are so many things in America I wish would die a natural death, so many things worthy of sarcasm it's hard to find time for them all. And what of the frightening possibility that there's only a finite amount of contempt possible in one's lifetime? If that's true, should I squander my sneers on my old girlfriends, cat food commercials and Joan Rivers? Should I save it all up for monumentally stupid events like the invasion of Grenada or *Flashdance*?

And with a person universally accepted as laughable, like William Buckley, Kissinger, or this new guy my girlfriend's going out with, is a sneer worth my time? Is my opinion but one more bitter drop in an ocean of words? And timing is so important.

I believe that Cabbage Patch dolls are stupid, and if you buy one you probably have severe emotional problems, but the dolls are all sold, Christmas is over. I missed the sarcasm boat.

So the next time you're in a cheap motel room, trying to unbolt some garish purple-and-green monstrosity, and there's nothing on the tube but the Brady Bunch, and your girlfriend would rather keep company with a Cabbage Patch doll than with you, think of me and the hard job I have to do. Then give a sneer. Remember: a sneer is a terrible thing to waste.

Recovering, 1/10/84

LIFE

Bicoastal

The advent of jet travel has caused a lot of changes in America, but the main effect has been to make every major city in the U.S. look like an airport. Since most places already look the same, I don't really know why we fly anywhere. Maybe it's a mysterious addiction to jet lag, I don't know, but the difference between one coast and the other is more a matter of personality than of architecture.

If you're flying to L.A., for example, once you touch down that's the last time your feet will touch the ground. Walking is considered a criminal action in L.A. Most people in California come from somewhere else. They moved to California so they could name their kids Rainbow or Mailbox, and purchase tubular Swedish furniture without getting laughed at. It's a tenet also in California that the fiber of your clothing is equivalent to your moral fiber. Your "lifestyle" (as they say) is your ethic. This means that in California you don't really have to do anything, except look healthy, think good thoughts and pat yourself on the back about what a good person you are. And waiters in California want to be called by their first name. I don't know why.

In New York, on the other hand, you're lucky if you get a waiter. People on the East Coast regard people west of, say, Philadelphia as either slightly cute or slightly repugnant, alien life forms. Any show that comes from out of town to New York invariably gets a review which says in effect, "They might like this stuff in Hicksville, but this is the Apple, kids. This is the eye of God."

Californians don't have that kind of arrogance, luckily, because they can't pay attention long enough to finish anything.

That's why so many Californians are consultants or producers, and so many people in the East are writers or directors. Never mind that most writers on the best-seller lists couldn't put a well-formed sentence together if you gave them the glue, or that the so-called "serious" writers only write about writers writing stories about writers writing stories, the two coasts are still the cultural power centers of America: books, theater and art in the East; movies, music and TV in the West. Those who wheel and deal in the commodity of entertainment in America are, by necessity, bicoastal, which is a nonconcept really, a feeble attempt to attach glamour to jet lag.

The airplane is just a big bus between airports. Once you're on board you're in Flyover Country, legally nowhere, flying over the vast in-between of the nation, where people live and work as the objects of scorn from both coasts, the poor suckers that soak up the nonsense of the bicoastals. And until they get limos in Omaha, and gossip columns in Denver, the power will stay where it is—among a handful of East and West Coast jerks who spend most of their time trying to keep track of time zones.

Waiting for a plane, 5/15/84

Time Zones

I live on the West Coast and nothing annoys me more than getting a phone call at seven in the morning from some friend or agent in New York, wanting to borrow something or clinch some deal. I always hang up the phone feeling ripped off, and no wonder—it's three hours later there. New Yorkers have had their coffee and their danish, they've read *USA Today* and *The Times*. They're on top of the world, and they've had a couple of hours to sort things out.

And when I finally hop out of bed at two o'clock and call East to take back everything I said in the stupor of half sleep, New Yorkers are gone for the day. They're out having cocktails, wearing tuxedoes, tangling with muggers, sampling the rich Manhattan night life. Time zones were created by the power elite of New York City to keep themselves as the cultural center of America. We don't need time zones.

Time is a fiction created by the government to make sure that trains and airplanes run on time. Time is a fiction created to sell digital watches. We have time only because businessmen want to go home *sometime*. The farmer doesn't need time. The sun comes up, and the farmer gets up; the sun goes down, and the farmer goes to bed. And for me, the opposite is true.

Time measurement, like the dictionary or telephone, is part of a conspiracy to make our lives more complicated in the guise of making our lives easier. Dictionaries were invented by stuffed shirts on a power trip, to tell us how and why a word should be used. I resent that. I resent telephones; an obnoxious loud noise tells us there's somebody on the line we wouldn't give the time of day to if we were standing face to face. And I hate time—take time, make time, get there on time, I don't have the time.

But what can I do against this tyrany? I can move to New York or unplug the phone. I can play the Eastern establishment's power game or smash my alarm. New York is cold, expensive, and I hate to fly. So bye bye Timex. See you later Touch-Tone. I'm going back to bed.

Under the covers, 9/12/82

Apartment Hunting

I gotta move, gotta go. I've been evicted. My personal stereo system, my Sears Silvertone with the green strings, my books. (I only have three books, *Movies on TV, Encyclopedia of Rock* and *Pale Fire.*) Once again I must pack my precious things and my black T-shirts into the trunk of somebody's car and find some place to live.

What kind of country is this where you can't bring home a half dozen good friends at four in the morning to listen to the new Ramones album? You *have* to play their music loud, and you have to talk louder if you're going to have any kind of intelligent conversation. It's a loud world, and you have to be loud to fit in.

Landlords don't understand this aesthetic. Landlords understand cockroaches; cockroaches are quiet and they'll sleep anywhere. Cockroaches are good tenants. So are people who get up in the morning, landlords love that kind of people. People who sing lusty songs at seven in the morning on the other side of paper-thin walls, people who listen to the *Today* show. The idea of Gene Shalit at any hour is more than I can take, but at dawn the idea is frightening. Landlords love Gene Shalit.

And there's nothing more disheartening than hunting through classifieds, driving from neighborhood to neighborhood, looking for signs in the windows. There's nothing more disheartening than realizing you're in your middle thirties and moving in with some twenty-two-year-old med student who doesn't smoke and doesn't want you to. I don't smoke myself, but I want the freedom to start if I choose. It's been almost twenty years of apartment hunting, ever since Dad kicked me out of the house, throwing my Velvet Underground records after me. I went to my girlfriend's house and asked if I could stay there. "Over my dead body," her Dad said. I understood his position. To paraphrase Groucho Marx: I wouldn't live anywhere that would let me live there.

On the road, May '83

What I Like

I know you people out there are mighty grateful to me for setting you straight on issues of cultural importance, and I'd like to thank you in turn for all the letters I get—

All right, it's just *one* letter, a *thankful* letter from Maryland, who likes my incisive comments but thinks I spend too much time on sarcasm and not enough on constructive criticism. This kind soul is worried about my emotional health and recommends, among other things, that I read the *Findhorn Garden Book* and take up horseback riding.

In response, let me say that I enjoy sarcasm, but I don't enjoy horses or gardens. Horses and gardens are large and lumpy, and you have to go outside to appreciate them. I don't go outside until the sun's set, that's the way I am. It's my responsibility to say No in a world that says Yes to every lame idea that comes down the pike. It's my destiny and my joy to tear down without building up.

But to make you feel better (I feel fine), let me share with you a few of the things I actually like about the modern world.

I like strong beer. I like animated cartoons—not those Oscar-winning political allegories from Hungary, but real cartoons with fuzzy animals trying to kill each other in cute ways. I like electric typewriters and answering machines; I like any machine I can turn off. I like the novels by Elmore Leonard and Thomas Pynchon. I like good sex if it doesn't last too long. I enjoy playing video games with other people's quarters. Like most Americans, I enjoy being afraid of Cuba. It's a harmless fear that makes America feel better and Cuba too. Cuba gets an inflated sense of national worth from the weight of our paranoia. I like getting large checks in the mail, especially if I've done nothing to earn them. I like the aroma of popcorn and women who like to hear me talk. I like to laugh at dogs. I like to call toll-free numbers and chat with the operators. I like phones that ring instead of chirp, clocks that have a face, Audie Murphy Westerns, duck *à l'orange* and onion rings, old movies on television, and every tenth video on MTV.

Reggae music, Motown and the songs of Randy Newman are an undiluted pleasure. I like the way rock singers pronounce the word baby—*Bay-Buh. Bay-Buh.* It never fails to amuse me. These are a few of my favorite things—about all of my favorite things. Make me feel real loose like a long-necked goose and—o-oh *bay buh*—that's what I like.

Reading my mail, 1/28/83

Cocaine

Cocaine. As a drug it compares favorably to novocaine, or any local anesthetic. It numbs the nose and the back of the throat, destroys the sinuses; increased usage leads to psychological dependence, wild mood swings, paranoia, delusions of grandeur, and even worse, delusions of intelligence. It's expensive, and it spills all over everything. So why do people use it?

Because cocaine is a tiny emblem of power held over another person. When someone gives you cocaine at a party, it means you have to stand and listen to him jabber for ten minutes. Coke users talk intensely about the most trivial things in the world, like brand names of audio equipment and video playback systems, and where they got their coke and how pure it is, and how hard it is to fly the stuff out of Bolivia. They go into a list of all the phone calls they've made that day, and all the projects they've got in the works. A little tiny bit of coke offered to me in the dark corner of a party tells me, "Wow, this useless person is giving me a little bit of this absolutely useless highly expensive thing." If someone set a hundred-dollar bill on fire in front of me, I would get the same thrill minus the boring coked-out conversation.

Cocaine culture: synthesizers, movies like *Cat People*, TV shows like *Fridays*, very shiny clothing, *Real Men Don't Eat Quiche*—the cute disguised as the cynical. Real men *do* eat quiche. Real money and real lives do go down the drain from cocaine, which isn't to say I wouldn't take some if it was offered to me. It keeps you awake at those boring parties, and gives you the illusion your opinions are worth something, as you beam and spew out intense and detailed critiques of *E.T.* or any other nonsense that pops into your teeming head.

By the time I actually saw *E.T.* at the drive-in I'd heard it recapped so many times at parties, the actual viewing experience seemed redundant. That's cocaine in a nutshell. Drive-ins used to mean something. Movies used to mean something.

I remember once when I was a kid we went to the drive-in. There was a shower of falling stars, and all of us got out of our cars to stand in the grass and watch the stars fall down. The movie was ignored behind us. When I saw *E.T.* at the drive-in, the sky was filled with roaring jets and the real estate around the drive-in was so developed that I spent half my time squinting from the bright headlights of cars blinding me as they hustled busily on their way to somewhere. It *is* a cocaine world, fast and smug, and self-conscious—like putting your face in the photocopy machine, then making a copy of that, a copy of that, copies inside copies, echoes inside echoes, until we've lost the original. We just hear a voice droning on and on. The only thing we see is our own face, nodding, reflecting in those French import mirror wraparound shades. Sunglasses in the dark. That's cocaine.

Spruce Drive-in, 6/12/82

Hobbies

Thirty years ago everyone had a hobby. Boys had the baseball cards, Sis had a thousand dolls from other lands, Mom had her yarn, Dad had his hi-fi kit, his woofers and tweeters. We'd assemble the jigsaw puzzle in the blond living room, listening to a freight train moan from speaker to speaker. Hobbies were the empire of the middle class, a strong nation taking its leisure, a strong family seeking temporary joy from solitary pleasures.

I'm not here to defend hobbies. I haven't had one since I was ten. I got a model Flying Fortress after seeing some John Garfield movie. I got the airplane glue, the decals, the small bottles of eye-damaging phosphorescent paint. I was trying to put Tab D into Slot Double Z when I spilled glue on the tail-gunner turret, at the exact point where John Garfield had shot down two Zeroes at twelve o'clock high. So I threw the damn thing across the garage, and blew it to smithereens on the Fourth of July with one well-placed cherry bomb. It was really cool, and I did it myself.

Hobbies today are a way to let the neighbors know how we fit in culturally. You're on top of the new, you've got the bucks to be hip. When Dad collected coins he didn't *interface* with anything, and when Mom made a quilt she didn't think she was experiencing a New Age Alternative Lifestyle. Hobbies used to be silly. Now there aren't any harmless ways to spend time. Video games gird our reflexes for war, prepare the young for Star Wars in the thin interface between blue sky and black space. We don't do anything for the hell of it. We have the hobby because the experts say we need to counter on-the-job stress, to counter executive burn-out (a real *maladie moderne*, the perfect disease for the '80s). We jog because we want to live longer, but the amount of time added to our lives is exactly equivalent to the time we spent jogging. We're big on choice but the choice is always twelve different episodes of *Three's Company*. We're a lonely nation of consumers, choosing our tired evenings away.

And the H-O trains that used to fill entire basements, all the miniature trees and park benches, the cute villages and villagers tiny as ants and bright as a promise of utopia. Those trains are gone; now we ride those trains. We take our tiny lives to our 9-to-5s, scanning the paper for computer bargains as we stand and rock, hemmed in by strangers. Now it's just a straight unbroken line from suburb to skyscraper, and everything is work.

On the Muni, 6/6/83

The Perfect City

If this were a perfect world we'd have at least one perfect city. The perfect city would look a bit like Fritz Lang's Metropolis, without the worker problems and without the electronic music. In the perfect city, big-band jazz would be broadcast nightly on the streets, which would be paved with bricks and lined with elm and maple trees.

The only dogs allowed would be African basenjis, which cannot bark and would be trained to curb themselves. All cars would float on silent cushions of air. All the cops would ride horses. There are no pigeons and no statues.

In the perfect city, automatic tellers would spew cash at random every half hour or so, the concerts would all be free, all be reggae music, and never be crowded. Drinks are half price, and it is always early autumn in the perfect city.

In the perfect city, Woody Allen would be funny again, Steven Spielberg would take a vacation, and there would be a Kurosawa festival once a month. Westerns would make a comeback, and theater seats would be six bucks tops. Critics would be wise, enthusiastic and fair, and so with the artists of the city. No art after 1900 would be displayed in the museums. Admission to museums would be free, and large groups of children would stay well away until I had left the building.

I would never be put on hold in the perfect city.

In the perfect city, all parties would be "by invitation only," and guests would receive cash prizes when they went through the door. I would be invited to all these parties, and no matter how rude I became, I would never be asked to leave.

In the perfect city there would be a twenty-four-hour French restaurant but all the entrées would be under five bucks. The waiters would be named Mac and the waitresses would all call you Honey.

In the perfect city, clothing would be well cut, sharp, swell and inexpensive. People would roam the streets in formal evening wear. In the perfect city, I would have a nickname like "Spats" or "Captain Danger." Every newsboy, flower seller, and cabbie would know my name; even the muggers would know my name. The mayor would call me for advice, my quips would be legendary in the society columns, the library would be well stocked, and super heroes and heroines would drift lazily among the skyscraper peaks, seeking out wrongdoers everywhere.

The shower in my apartment would be hot and powerful, and all my neighbors would work nights. Women would laugh at my jokes, and men wouldn't tell them. Guitars would stay in tune. I would have many friends, and they would not ask me for money. They would all have jobs, and their jobs would be good. I would have my own news program, in which I would bring bad news to the perfect city, but nobody would mind, because everybody would know I had a bad attitude anyway.

Women would stay with me longer than two months, or if they left they'd at least leave their record collections, which would include all recordings by the Ramones. And they'd leave me a record player. And some money.

All transportation is free, including tickets out of town. And down those mean streets a man would go, who was not himself afraid, and that would be me, the oldest pro on the block. Ian "Captain Danger" Shoales. In the perfect city.

Watching the pigeons, 10/15/84

MILESTONES

Heart Man

Family souvenirs. The flotsam and jetsam that toss on the dusty tide of mothballs and stale air in attics across the nation. The debris: snapshots of Johnny age three feeding Kleenex to the cat, Jill age four in her crinoline and Sunday shoes, slides of a waterfall in Kentucky with Mom, Dad and Gramps in their out-of-focus grins obscuring what beauty may once have been in a tourist-destroyed American landscape. Scrapbooks: yellow clippings of Janey's wedding, Tommy's tragic accident, the family reunion photos—dozens of relatives whose names you no longer remember, standing in a clump at the end of a large room, staring grimly at the camera, their arms hanging stiffly at their sides.

Nobody takes pictures of the family anymore. Now it's all videotapes of baby crawling, videotapes of weddings and birthday parties. Hours and hours of family activity so dull and pointless they bring to mind the worst of Andy Warhol.

The icons of family history are fast being replaced by images of the Global Village. The doings of Liz are much more interesting than the doings of Mom.

That's why I followed with great interest the homey coverage given to the late Dr. Barney Clark, the media-styled Heart Man. Once weekly on page 10, say, of your local daily, you'd see a five-line news release with a headline like "Heart Man Sits Up," or "Heart Man Watches Television," or "Heart Man Says Complete Sentence." It took a medical miracle—the world's first artificial heart—to bring back those bland touching details that used to grace our scrapbooks and home movies.

You never saw "Heart Man Gets Divorce," or "Heart Man Lands New Series" or "Heart Man Tells Reporters to Get the

Hell out of His Room." It was always "Heart Man Reads Magazine." "Heart Man Smells Flowers." "Heart Man Takes Three Steps, Then Rests."

Today, of course, artificial-heart recipients, like astronauts, are old hat: "Oh, we went to the moon *again?*" Tomorrow, no doubt, artificial hearts will be reserved only for the very rich, aging burnt-out rock stars, or eccentric self-made millionaires. Or maybe the recipients will be selected by national lottery.

To America, Dr. Clark was the pioneer, all the others are just copycats. But his story wasn't the story of a bland superhero, it wasn't the Heart Man Chronicles. Those tiny articles were there to fill space, just the perfect size to clip and paste in a scrapbook. He was just an amiable man with an artificial heart, trying his best to live a natural life.

Reading the paper, 2/26/85

Scandalized

Miss America naked. Oh boy, another scandal. As we get more and more sophisticated, and more and more lawyers, paradoxically we get easier and easier to shock. It used to take a movie star found on the yacht with an under-age girl, or a public official caught in the wading pool with an exotic dancer, now James Watt trying to remove his foot from his mouth, or a lovely black woman revealing her body for photographers gets the same gasp of breath as the resignation of a President. What happened to scandals?

Joan Rivers at the Emmies, remember that? Vanessa Redgrave or Marlon Brando at the Oscars. Mountains out of molehills. Marlon Brando is a real molehill. All our celebrities are molehills. There hasn't been a decent flap in this country since the Vicki Morgan sex tapes.

Admit it. You haven't watched the Miss America Pageant since they canned Bert Parks. And you haven't picked up a

Penthouse since they rejected your letter about that interesting experience you had with that stewardess in a New York Toll Plaza in 1981. I'm not going to plug in my TV again, or shell out a couple of bucks to Bob Guccione, the Caligula of girlie magazines. This isn't a scandal at all. There weren't any kickbacks or break-ins—just a black woman who took off her clothes for money. She made an error in judgment, a mistake that might make her a stronger person.

What can they do to her? The Miss America crown is a badge of wholesomeness. Can she have wholesomeness stripped from her, like badges from a disgraced official? Will they take away her swimsuit and dorky high heels? Or conversely, will Bob Guccione become the new Bert Parks, with his light meter and gold chain, trying to persuade Miss Congeniality to remove a few things in the back seat of his gold Rolls Royce? I doubt it, but then again, in a nation where a Playboy can have a philosophy and Larry Flynt can run for President, anything is possible.

I think it will blow over in a couple weeks. It won't even get a *-gate* or *-scam* attached to the end of it, like a big-league scandal. It's barely worthy of the *National Enquirer*, in whose pages lawsuits are as common as weight-loss programs. Scandals are on the down-swing. Nobody wants to tell a whopper, just point to a little molehill. There are too many lawyers. Litigation has led to a failure of the imagination.

Miss America meets *Penthouse*. It's a media collision between two false images of the American woman, and bland images to boot. The bland lead the bland in this country. We're supposed to think it's tragic that Miss America got sexy. A black woman got to be just as bland as the rest of white America, and she threw it away. But I think it's for the best. Vanessa Williams will be naked in the spotlight for a moment, then put on her clothes and go on with her life. Take it from me, Vanessa. America's better off. Miss America has a body now. And *Penthouse* will sell a lot of magazines. That's the bland truth.

At the newsstand, August '84

Grand Illusions

The first public event that had any personal effect on me was undoubtedly the breakup of Dean Martin and Jerry Lewis. I looked forward to the change, actually. Dean Martin was always popcorn time in my book, and two hours of Jerry Lewis solo seemed to epitomize an eight-year-old's paradise.

Today, of course, in a nation inured to humor by the college-boy mentality of *Animal House*, or the smart mouth leering of *Saturday Night Live*, you have to go all the way to France even to see a Jerry Lewis movie. But when I was a kid, if you wanted to be my pal you said nothing bad about Jerry Lewis, and if your favorite third stooge wasn't Shemp it was Fist City.

What do kids love today? They can't breakdance at the mall. Girl Scout cookies are filled with razor blades. Hallowe'en has become a killing zone for psychopaths, and the only comedians worth anything in this country have this peculiar desire to act like grown-ups. I can sympathize with Steve Martin. He must wake up sweating in the middle of the night, imagining himself as an eighty-year-old man being wheeled around the home with an arrow through his head, saying "I'm a wild and crazy guy" over and over again. But still, there's a place in America for pure pagan physical humor. Not every Jerry Lewis has to become Dean Martin, not every Woody Allen has to make sincere movies about relationships.

You don't have to sneer at Jerry Lewis now, or feel ashamed that you loved him when you were a kid. Nostalgia might be the final refuge for people who hate what they've become, but don't throw your memories out with the bathwater. If you like a pie in the face, say so. You don't have to cover up your appreciation of something stupid by calling it camp, or hiding your delight under so many levels of irony you couldn't cut through it with a chain saw. Save your irony for when you really need it.

I remember on my eighth birthday, in compensation for a painful trip to the orthodontist, my parents took me to the Marshall Bill show, a so-called kiddy program which aired live every weekday between three and three-thirty in an unnamed Midwestern state. It was a minor thrill to be there among Porky and his pals, sitting in my Cub Scout uniform on Marshall Bill's birthday saddle. Even though at eight years old I was a bit long in the tooth to experience much more than subdued embarrassment, still it *was* my birthday.

Marshall Bill gave me a birthday badge, and a gift certificate for a genuine ant farm. The ant farm arrived in the mail six weeks later. All the ants, of course, were dead, which may have been the first in a series of my disillusionments with the American way of life. On the other hand, I always knew that Santa Claus was really Vern Halstad, the insurance man three houses down, the Tooth Fairy was Mom with a dime; I always knew that cartoons were created by fat guys in white shirts and unlit cigars, that cameras were operated by bored men with permanent yawns, and Jerry Lewis the kid was really a grown man who smoked too much.

And I always knew that Marshall Bill was really just the local weatherman with a cowboy hat. That didn't diminish my appreciation for their service. You must accept human frailty in the world. You gotta go with the grand illusions. After all, I'm just a weatherman myself—you know, the kind that knows which way the wind blows. And just for the record: my favorite third stooge is still Shemp.

After watching The King of Comedy, *7/9/84*

Paper Wings

Before my voice changed, some twenty-odd years ago, I was a mediocre boy soprano, and every Christmas it was the custom for the good Reverend Crabb to trot me out, all decked out in sheet, tinsel and coat-hanger halo to portray the herald angel for the Sabbath gathering. I would stand before the congregation between three fifth-grade boys in papier-maché beards and the rather gaudy plaster statues representing the Holy Family, and I would sing the third verse of "O Holy Night" in as pure a tenor as ever I will have, accompanied on a vast and gleaming pipe organ by Marianne Gunderson, a high-school senior with a reputation for being a bit wild.

It wouldn't have worked out between me and Marianne. I was twelve and she was eighteen, for one thing, but as she watched me there in church, the paper wings on my back were quivering as if possessed of a sluggish long-dormant desire to fly. This had a peculiar effect on my mental state. I was both exalted and embarrassed. Embarrassed because I was dressed like a paper angel in the presence of Marianne Gunderson, and exalted because, after all, we were making music together. Time stood still. All time zones ceased to exist. All the grown-ups in the congregation had that peculiar smile adults get when they are in the presence of something cute—the Reverend Crabb was smiling, my parents were smiling, everybody was smiling, even the Christ child in a plaster kind of way.

The ice on the moment thawed. We went on to the Doxology and Recessional, then back through the cold winter to our homes. My voice changed that summer, Marianne went to college—you know how time goes. The plaster family is still dusted off once a year, and I'll bet the angel this year is *hot*, and the girl on the organ has magenta streaks in her hair and a reputation for being a bit wild.

That's time for you. Human pleasure and sorrow are each flip sides of the other. We might be fallen angels or apes who've learned to cry, I don't know, I only indulge in that kind of speculation when there's nothing on television, but I do know that life is a dream of flying. We all carry our paper wings as we dream along, a silly tender burden to remind us that the blessings that flow in life are always mixed blessings, but we still gotta count them, as best we can.

Waiting for Santa, 12/24/84

THE IAN SHOALES SCRAPBOOK

The Making of a Social Critic

I'm one of those people who went to school until I couldn't get any more degrees. Young people today can benefit from my ten years of college, so here's some advice.

- Avoid any course called Colonial American Literature. You will read smug creeps like Benjamin Franklin, psychotics like Edgar Allan Poe, half-smart mystics like Ralph Waldo Emerson, and turgid pulp writers like James Fenimore Cooper. American Literature in general is not worth the paper it's printed on.
- Henry James will put you to sleep in seconds.
- Avoid psychology. Sigmund Freud was a half-baked Viennese quack. Our literature, culture, and the films of Woody Allen would be better today if Freud had never written a word. Also ignore B. F. Skinner and behaviorism, a school of psychology that reduces experience to a meaningless series of manipulations, punishments and rewards.
- Steer clear of existentialism, a morbid philosophy based on unprovable premises, designed solely so graduate students can sprout ratty little beards, drink strong coffee till 3 A.M. and come to believe that despair is sexually appealing. It's not. Even if despair were sexy, the people you meet in philosophy classes aren't. And Jean-Paul Sartre was a third-rate thinker whose pathetic attempts at irony were done much better on *The Twilight Zone*. If you wish to appeal to the opposite sex (the prime reason for higher education)—or the same sex, as far as that goes—buy nice clothes and join a fraternity or sorority.

- Ernest Hemingway is the most overrated writer who ever lived.
- If you're a young person who writes poetry, throw it all away. Right now. Unless it's Christmas-card verse, there is no money in poetry.
- Never take film classes. In a film class you will never see a movie that is even remotely entertaining, and even if you did, it would be talked to death by various graduate students with theoretical axes to grind.
- Writing classes are all taught by over-the-hill beatniks who will bore you to death with monotonous stories about their drinking days with Jack Kerouac. You will never get an agent in a writing class.
- Don't read, skim.
- If you are unlucky enough to get in a class that requires a term paper, sprinkle your essay with these words:

Interface	Hermetic
Relevance	Discourse
Dialectic	Admirable
Hermeneutics	Taxonomy

- The word "stupid" is never allowed by a teacher as a critical response to a work of art.

The best advice I can give young people today is: fail. Fail now, while you're young enough to enjoy it. Failure is a virtue in today's society. Human error is a badge of honor. Don't learn from your mistakes, embrace your mistakes. A failure is a success.

If you make a mistake and admit it, you're a good sport. If you make a mistake and blame it on someone else, you're a good politician. If you make a mistake and admit it aggressively and frequently, people will come to believe that your mistake was the Right Move and you will be elected senior-class president and go straight to Harvard.

If you're the formerly alcoholic offspring of a celebrity, you can blame your mistakes on your celebrity parent and earn yourself a year on the best-seller lists. If you're a celebrity in your own right, your mistakes could earn you a *People* Magazine cover, just in time to plug your network special. On the network special your mistakes will be called *embarrassing moments* or *bloopers* and can get you up to an hour of prime time, throwing your mistakes out for the viewing enjoyment of millions. If you become addicted to drugs or alcohol, kick the habit. If you can kick the habit, the world is your oyster—best sellers, seminars, speaking engagements, all to help people learn from your mistakes. But first you have to make them.

In a bizarre parody of evolution, human error these days is rewarded handsomely. Everybody takes the credit for success, but only one person usually takes the blame. In any bureaucracy there is always a scapegoat. If you're the scapegoat, write a book about it, or sue somebody. This is the trickle-down theory of punishment and blame. This is post-Watergate morality. The fittest are the unfit. Take responsibility for your mistakes, and you can make a quick buck.

If you make a mistake the world is your oyster. There's a danger that the meek might inherit that oyster, so you might as well eat it now. Why should the meek get it? They're a bunch of wimps. If you don't like oysters, become a lawyer. Lawyers always make money, no matter who's to blame.

Remember kids, all great art is boring. Dress well and drink a lot. That's what college is all about. Become a lawyer or a doctor. Every other profession is just too iffy. I ought to know.

It's too late for me. Ever since my high-school principal sued me for libel, the course of my life has been set. While nobody has ever broken down and admitted publicly that he or she admired me and everything I stood for, I'm sure there must be somebody out there interested in my personal history. Yes, now that you know where I'm coming from, let's see where I've been. Let's turn back the pages of time and display the roots of the brilliant yet arrogant man the world knows as Ian Shoales.

In the attic, 3/25/84

OK

your work is much neater
than it was before.

Ian Shoales Nov. 7, 195

Story Report

Title: The Box That Quentin
Carved.

Author: L. Lamprey

This story is about a boy
named Quentin who loved to whittle
more than anything else. He was
in Chicago when a building fell on
his father. How he managed to work while
his father was in the hospital
you'll have to find out for yourself.
It's a stupid story just because
we're kids we have to read this
junk. And why do we have to make
Q's look like Z's? And K's look
like B's. I think the Palmer
method is stupid too. The story can be found on
page 8 of the Living all Your
Life books. I have to go.

JUNIOR HIGH JABBERS

olume 2, Number 2   Woodrow Wilson Junior High School

'TWAS THE NIGHT BEFORE CHRISTMAS
by Ian Shoales

'was the night before Christmas
and all through the house,
ot a creature was stirring, not
even a mouse.

woke from my slumber and gave a
small shout.
ould it be that a burglar was
crawling about?

reached for my shotgun and
went down the stair,
nd hoped that a burglar wouldn't
be there.

A shadowy figure! My gun gave a
boom!
The echo resounded throughout the
large room.

The poor fellow lay there among all
his toys.
I heard my wife shouting and cries
of the boys.

With a Barbie doll stuck in his
pink paws,
Dead on the floor lay poor Santa
Claus.

LIBRARY

We now have 283 new books. All
these should be handled with care
d consideration for others who
ay like to read them.

Some of the new nonfiction books
at would really be worth reading
are *Black Jack Pershing; Ike Eisen-
hower, Statesman and Soldier of Peace;
Meet Soviet Russia; Franklin D. Roosevelt;* all books by Dr. Thomas A.
Dooley; and *Profiles in Courage.*

Ian Shoales
English 421
Dr. Graves

STANLEY EDGAR HYMAN ON NATHANIEL WEST'S *MISS LONELYHEARTS*: THE CRITICISM OF REDUCTION.

At first glance, Stanley Edgar Hyman seems to have given *Miss Lonelyhearts* an intelligent and lucid treatment. A second glance, however, reveals a paucity of vision on Hyman's part.

Ian Shoales
Cinema as Dramatic Art
Dr. Fisher

PAULINE KAEL ON ANTONIONI'S *BLOW-UP:* THE CRITICISM OF REDUCTION.

At first glance, Pauline Kael seems to have given *Blow-Up* an intelligent and lucid treatment. A second glance, however, reveals a paucity of vision on Kael's part.

Ian Shoales
Dramatic Theory and Criticism
Mr. Frees

RUDOLF ARNHEIM'S *FILM AS ART:* THE CRITICISM OF REDUCTION.

At first glance, Rudolf Arnheim seems to have given films an intelligent and lucid treatment. A second glance, however, reveals a paucity of vision on Arnheim's part.

Ian Shoales
Anthropology 121
Miss Mudd

MARGARET MEAD ON SAMOA: THE CRITICISM OF REDUCTION.

At first glance, Margaret Mead seems to have given Samoa

Intro to the National Writer's Test   Finally I offer this lump in the landscape of my personality. I got the National Writer's Test in the mail two years ago. I spent a couple minutes (during commercials) filling it out and sending it back. I never received a reply.

I offer it here to you now for two reasons. One, to show the intrinsic evil of bulk mailing permits; and two, to tell you more about me than you could possibly want to know.

National Writer's Test

Why a National Writer's Test?   Many fledgling writers ask us this question. We don't have an answer, but we have another question: wouldn't *you* take a test that has existed since 1933, formulated by psychological experts and experienced writers, in sterile laboratory conditions, for the sole purpose of determining, with pinpoint accuracy, your ability to write material that sells?

Of course you would. Naturally we can't guarantee your success (that depends upon your personal ambition and stick-to-it-iveness), but we can show you whether you *can* write.

Science has shown that the need for self-expression is genetic. If there's a Shakespeare or Jackie Collins somewhere in your DNA, we'll roll up our sleeves and find him or her for you. As they say in logic, if you can write you can write. The rest is just packaging.

We'll help you find out if you have the right personality, the right temperament, and the right agent. If you pass this test, our professional mail-order instructors will help you expand your limits (for a fee), help you make the most of what little or lot you have.

What is the National Writer's Test?   This is another commonly asked question. Well, we reply, the test has six sections, each with a different function. The first section tells us a little bit about you: your height and weight, your likes and dislikes, how much money you make, and your ability to obey instructions while observing others.

The other sections are subtle psychological probes devised by our editorial department, who spent months preparing them. They worked overtime on this one, and we suggest you do the same.

The sections are here to measure you, and all replies will be held in the strictest confidence. Answer every question, no matter how intimate or strange it seems. We know what we're doing. Trust us. And if you should begin to receive bizarre mail-order offers over the next four to six weeks, and continue to receive them for the rest of your life, don't worry. This is because we sell our mailing list to other organizations. This practice in no way reflects your ability (or nonability) to write.

You may, if you choose, enclose a writing sample with your completed test. We will be as careful as we can with it, but cannot assume liability for loss of your sample, nor will we promise to read it.

How Will I Do on the National Writer's Test?   Patience. We cannot tell until you have *completed* the National Writer's Test. We will only say that nobody has failed yet, and we will offer you some advice.

Write as though you were writing to a close friend, your best friend from high school, say, or (if you aren't on speaking terms with your high-school friend) a friend from work. Think of us as a lover whom you haven't seen in years, but would like to see again. Yes, think of us as your lover or friend. Don't think of us as a stranger here at the National Writer's Test. We have been around the block a few times. As such, we are sincere, fun-loving (yet respectful), and have been known to have a beer or two when the working day is done.

When Will I Take the National Writer's Test?   Questions, questions, questions! Just one more comment and then we'll get out of your way. The analysis of your test results will cost you nothing. Should our report be accompanied by an invitation to join us here at the National Writer's Test, to become one of the gang, to shoot the breeze over a beer or two when the working day is done, you do not have to accept that invitation. If you want to go home and watch television, or if you have some previous engagement, or some chores you need to complete, that's all right with us. You are under no obligation, none at all. There's no problem. No pressure. Do what you want. We got along without you before you took the National Writer's Test, and we can get along without you after you took it too. You're only hurting yourself.

The Ten Leading Creative Indicators Determined by the National Writer's Test:

1. Your sense of narrative
2. Your sense of humor
3. Your sense of personality
4. Your ability to type
5. Your ability to purchase an electric typewriter
6. Your software
7. Your imagination
8. Your ancestry
9. Your ability to take orders without complaint
10. Your checking account

Section One

CONFIDENTIAL INFORMATION

We cannot help you unless you help us first. Do not assume that all these answers affect our judgment as to your writing ability. Assume nothing. We are tricky, but we are fair.

NAME ...... Ian Shoales ....

ADDRESS ...... PO 22513 SF CA 94122 ....

OCCUPATION ...... Acerbic Social Critic ....

HOBBIES ...... I don't have any hobbies ....

AGE ...... 36 ....

HEIGHT ...... 5'11" ....   WEIGHT ...... 160 ....

SEX ...... Infrequent and dissatisfying ....

WHAT MAGAZINES HAVE YOU READ IN THE LAST MONTH?
Harper's, GQ, W, New Yorker. I'd read more but there's no room in my apartment for a coffee table.

WHAT TELEVISION PROGRAMS HAVE YOU SEEN IN THE LAST MONTH?
People's Court and a three a.m. screening of *The Falcon's Brother* with George Sanders and Tom Conway. Good movie. Wish you'd been there to watch it with me.

WHAT KIND OF READING DO YOU MOST ENJOY?
Tabloids and the backs of cereal boxes.

NAME TEN OF YOUR FAVORITE AUTHORS.
Joseph Smith. Isak Dinesen. Flannery O'Connor. Vladimir Nabokov. M. R. James. A. Conan Doyle. Charles Dickens. Roland Barthes. Ellery Queen. Erich Von Däniken.

HAVE YOU WRITTEN ANYTHING WHICH YOU HAVE NOT TRIED TO PUBLISH?

My 1,500 page rock-and-roll novel.

HAVE YOU EVER BEEN PUBLISHED?

Yes.

IF SO, GIVE SPECIFICS.

No.

HAVE YOU EVER WRITTEN FOR A NEWSPAPER?

Yes.

IF SO, WHAT?

My column, "Stop the War Machine."

WHAT NEWSPAPER?

Stop the War Machine.

WHEN?

During the *war.*

ARE YOU A GOOD JUDGE OF HUMAN NATURE?

I hope not.

DO YOU ENJOY STUDYING HUMAN NATURE?

No.

ANIMALS?

Huh?

NATURE?

Haw.

CHILDREN?

Forget it.

ARE YOU SOCIALLY ACTIVE?

Yes.

INACTIVE?

When I'm asleep.

IF YOU HAVE TRAVELED, STATE BRIEFLY WHERE.

All over.

WHAT IS YOUR FAVORITE COLOR?

I hate colors.

ARE YOU MARRIED?
> Why? Are you?

IF NOT, DO YOU PLAN TO BE MARRIED SOON?
> What are *you* doing after the test?

HOW MANY STATE CAPITALS CAN YOU NAME, WITHOUT LOOK-ING?
> Thirty-five.

WOULD YOU BE INTERESTED IN WORKING FOR AN OUT-OF-TOWN NEWSPAPER?
> How far out of town?

DO YOU THINK THERE IS LIFE AFTER DEATH?
> What *are* you doing after the test?

WHAT'S YOUR FAVORITE SPORT?
> Strangling mimes.

HAVE YOU EVER WRITTEN A LETTER TO A MEN'S MAGAZINE?
> Just to Ann Landers.

WHAT ARE YOUR SECRET FANTASIES?
> I don't have any.

WHAT KIND OF CAR DO YOU DRIVE?
> A friend's.

DO YOU OWN ANY CREDIT CARDS?
> I can borrow them.

HOW MUCH MONEY DO YOU MAKE A YEAR?
> It's in the four figure department.

PLEASE ENCLOSE ALL TAX STATEMENTS FOR THE PAST FIVE YEARS.
> I burned them.

WHICH OF THE FOLLOWING ARE YOU MOST INTERESTED IN WRIT-ING? (NUMBER IN ORDER OF PREFERENCE 1 THROUGH 10, 10 THE LOWEST).

SHORT STORIES	No $ in it.
ARTICLES	1

POETRY	No $ in it.
TV/RADIO SCRIPTS	1
MOVIE SCRIPTS	1
STAGE PLAYS	No $ in it.
NOVELS	1
DIET BOOKS	10
COOK BOOKS	10
SEX FANTASIES	150
INTERVIEWS WITH STARS	30,000

DO YOU WANT TO DISCOVER WHAT PHASE OF WRITING IS BEST SUITED TO YOUR NATURAL ABILITIES?

No. I want to make money.

Section Two

DEVELOPING AN EYE FOR DETAIL

Our staff of artists collaborated on this depiction of an ordinary household event. Use the space below to write a complete account of your version of what is happening in this picture.

Keep in mind the law of the print medium: a picture is worth a thousand words, but a thousand words can be worth one libel suit. When you ask those ancient questions, "Who? What? Where? Why? When? and How?" make sure you consult a lawyer and verify your sources. The purpose of this test is to find out how well you can look at things. This can come in handy when you're a writer, believe us.

This test has another function, but it cannot be revealed to you at this time.

You're starting to baffle me here, National Writer's Test. In the first place, I don't like the way this picture is drawn, and in the second place this seems like some kind of psychological test. I don't like psychology. I don't like people who like psychology, unless we're talking Wilhelm Reich. *Are* we talking Wilhelm Reich? *Are* you married?

Section Three

CAN YOU HANDLE YOUR WORDS?

The Right Word for the Right Job

Words are the writer's stock in trade, his ace in the hole. If you can't handle them, you'd better cash in your chips and fold. So, circle the most appropriate word for each of the following sentences.

1. The pink house had matching _____ shutters.

   PINK (DISHEARTENED) HISTORICAL APPROPRIATE

2. The young thief was out of breath from _____.

   PANTING STEALING RUNNING (NEW JERSEY)

94

3. The number of roads a man may walk down before they call him a man is _____ in the wind.

TWELVE   (TWENTY)   UNKNOWN   BLOWING

4. The dictionary is full of _____.

PHANTOMS   WORDS   DUST   (MISTAKES)

5. A fierce _____ played about Tarzan's lips.

GRIN   (LION)   SCOWL   JANE

6. The cannibals threw up their hands in _____.

DESPAIR   AFRICA   DISREPUTE   (TANDEM)

7. Dr. Brown let out a _____ of derision.

SNORT   LION   MOUSE   (CREAM SODA)

8. The novels of Robert Ludlum are _____.

(LONG)   UBIQUITOUS   TRUE-TO-LIFE   HELPFUL

9. For your free pocket calculator call this toll-free _____.

WOMAN   NUMBER   BOOTH   (AMAZING)

10. This amazing television offer is not available in any _____.

(SENSE)   IRONY   STORE   NUMBER

Know Your Derivatives!

From the ancient Greek, the Latin word "mission" originally meant "of or pertaining to Spanish architecture." Later it came to mean "hideous responsibility" or "Americans who tell small countries what to do." The word "mission" has been incorporated into our language (English) in many forms (see below).

Select the proper word for the proper sentence.

MISSION   EMISSION
SUBMISSION   DISMISSAL
ADMISSION   RATIOCINATION

1. The voice on the tape informed Mr. Phelps about his impossible SUBMISSION _____ then self-destructed.

2. Bones looked grim, then made the predictable SUBMISSION _____, "He's dead, Jim."

95

3. The Starship *Enterprise* had a five-year SUBMISSION which included exploring strange new worlds, among other things.

4. "I don't know, Watson," said Holmes in a remarkable feat of SUBMISSION .

5. O. knelt trembling before her cruel mistress, in an attitude of RATIOCINATION .

6. These new SUBMISSION control standards only give us five miles to the gallon.

Section Four

CREATIVITY

We have written a story. Fill in the blanks with the most suitable words from your vocabulary. In the space provided at the bottom of the page, briefly describe what you think will happen.

I am a SOCIAL CRITIC at a large CRITICAL FACILITY . I was CRITICIZING late at the CRITICAL FACILITY when I heard a knock at the door. Imagine my surprise when I saw the SILLIEST AMERICAN I had ever seen.

He/She said, "I'm having a little trouble with my CULTURE and I was hoping you could help."

I'm always willing to help out a(n) AMERICAN . I followed him/her to his/her COLLECTIVE UNCONSCIOUS , where he/she made the startling and sly admission that it wasn't his/her CULTURE he/she was having trouble with at all but his/her FUTURE !

We'd had a few drinks by that point and I said, "I'm sure I can help you."

With a bold grin I slowly removed his/her SELF-DELU-SIONS . He/She had the biggest LIES ABOUT HIS/HER SELF I had ever seen! Well, needless to say, we were soon

CREATING A FUTURE STRIPPED OF MISCONCEPTIONS AND HALF-TRUTHS, FACING A PERFECT WORLD TOGETHER AND MAKING LOTS OF MONEY .

Section Five

FUN WITH CAPTIONS!

Study these four pictures. Then write the word or phrase
which best describes your mood. Many major newspapers
pay thousands of dollars for people to do this.

1. Nature's Uncontrollable Fury.
2. Barely Repressed Hysteria.
3. Free Floating Anxiety.
4. Pathological Psychosis.

Section Six

FORMULA FOR SUCCESS

We here at the National Writer's Test do a lot of research. That part of the job comes with the National Writer's Test territory. We try to keep up with what's happening in the publishing world. In drugstores and airports throughout the land we made a selection of paperbacks available to the American reader. Below you will see this selection combined into one condensation, a superplot. Read this superplot, which we have titled "The Armageddon Factor," then answer the questions which follow. You have thirty minutes left in the time allotted to you. Begin now.

THE ARMAGEDDON FACTOR

Lean Bob Hawkins held his Uzi in a nervous grip of iron. Across the remodeled kitchen his sultry wife, Astrid, with whom he had once (he remembered bitterly) had marital difficulties, returned his unflinching gaze with an answering look of support. This world crisis had, paradoxically, brought them closer together. They were waiting for Dmitri, Bob's ancient enemy and head of the dreaded KGB. There was a shapely tension, Bob admitted ruefully, to Astrid as she nervously stirred the *gazpacho* and leafed anxiously through a large thin volume of cats.

Had it only been moments before that they had had passionate sex together there on the parquet kitchen floor? *Yes,* he remembered, *yes.* He savored the memory. How they had fallen into each other's arms in the middle of their aerobics session, how they had drowned out the screams of the werewolves below them in the streets of Manhattan, drowned them out with sensuous moans of pleasure, with the loud strains of a rock LP, how they had experienced the bliss of short-term memory loss with the sickly sweet aroma of marijuana, and the powerful odors of their lithe sweating bodies. And Jason, thought Bob, coming back to the present with an ironic shudder. What will happen to him if we fail?

He had shouldered all thoughts of failure from his mind

when Dmitri burst through the door. Bob grimly caught him in the shoulder with a burst from his Uzi. Dmitri slid slowly to the floor, a thin line of blood trickling from the corner of his mouth.

"Farewell, respected enemy," muttered Dmitri in Ukrainian, breathing his last. Astrid clutched Bob and breathed, "It's horrible, Bob, horrible."

"But it's over," said Bob.

"Not quite," came a voice from the shadows.

"You!" shouted Bob and Astrid. It was dark and troubled Jake Gleeson who stepped into the room, the deadly crossbow held level at his waist. Bob realized as he raised his hands that it had been Jake all along: Jake his best friend, Jake the double agent, Jake who had released the top-secret virus that killed half the world's population and turned the other half into sex-crazed psychotics or werewolves, Jake who had muttered the secret incantation which released the blood-maddened demons Father Kreisler had given his life to stop. Bob remembered the crusty priest winking as he died, drained by his exorcism, a trickle of blood moving slowly from the corner of his thin drawn lips. What use are my skills as a *ninja* journalist now? thought Bob helplessly.

But the insane smile of power and triumph froze on Jake's lips as a shot rang out. Jake crumpled at their feet, a thin line of blood trickling from the corner of his mouth. Behind him, the .44 Magnum still smoking in his tiny hands, stood three-year-old blond Jason, their son.

"I had to, Daddy," he said and began to cry.

"It's okay, honey," soothed Astrid in that self-confident way she had developed since this world crisis had brought them all, paradoxically, closer together.

As Astrid trundled Jason off to bed, Bob, hunched with exhaustion, flesh wounds, and the weight of the world he had saved, dialed the secret number of the President. It was true, he thought with bitterness, that the scars Jason had gained over these past five days of terror would never heal, but still, there were the finishing touches on that letter to the *New York Times,* there was that diet book to write, and tomorrow? Tomorrow was another day.

QUESTIONS

1. DOES THIS HAVE THE MAKINGS OF A BOOK YOU MAY READ ON
AN AIRPLANE OR WAITING IN LINE AT THE GROCERY STORE?
Sure.

2. DID YOU FIND ANY SIGNIFICANCE IN THE AUTHOR'S USE OF
NUMBERS, COLOR AND SPACE? WHY OR WHY NOT?
No.

3. WHERE DO YOU THINK THIS APARTMENT IS AND HOW MUCH
RENT DO YOU THINK THEY PAY?
You *must* be married.

4. WHAT IS THE PURPOSE OF IMAGINATION?
To make money.

5. CAN THERE BE KNOWLEDGE WITHOUT EXPERIENCE?
No.

6. HOW MUCH DO YOU KNOW? (BE CAREFUL ON THIS ONE.)
Enough to get by.

7. HAS A WILD ANIMAL EVER CROSSED *YOUR* PATH? WRITE YOUR
OWN BEST SELLER, USING YOUR OWN EXPERIENCES.
I knew it. This isn't going to make me any money.

Dates

There's a new magazine called *One Woman*, and the entire ninety-six pages of its first issue will be devoted to the wit, wisdom and figure of Morgan Fairchild. If it sells, *One Woman* will appear quarterly with a different woman per issue. *One Woman* is the logical extension of monogamy, computer mania, and the lingering death of the printed word. A picture used to be worth a thousand words, and now a thousand words are worth one picture. You need ninety-six pages to examine someone you wish you forgot. Morgan Fairchild isn't a woman, she's a corporate merger, a public-relations stroke. And she wouldn't date you in a million years.

All right I admit it. I have trouble with women. They don't go out with me, and if they do go out with me they don't do it twice. And I'll admit that my idea of a good time is hitchhiking to a Ramones concert, followed by a malt-liquor nightcap and a chili dog at 4 A.M. Many women don't appreciate the fun of this.

But I've got something to offer a woman—a unique world view and a genuine if stunted sensuality—and I'm sure there's a woman out there with something to offer me. So let me give you guys advice about women:

> Don't date a woman news anchor. She'll have that Dear Abby hair that will snap off her head when you touch it.
> Don't date a woman who writes articles for *Cosmopolitan*. She's looking for a husband and career to juggle. If you're only after one thing, which I frankly am, you're barking up the wrong tree.

Avoid all women writers, as a matter of fact. They're probably smarter and have more problems than you. And women writers, like male writers, don't know how to have fun.

Never date a woman with only one name, like Alana, or Sunrise, or Cherri, or Rainbow. Don't do it pal, you're only asking for trouble.

Never date a woman with three names. Women with three names are almost always poets, and when the relationship breaks up (as it inevitably will), these women will write nasty poems about you that will be anthologized for years to come, poems that will haunt you in public libraries from coast to coast. Never write a poem for a woman. Women remember things like that and will hold it against you when you eventually betray them.

Never date a woman who won't fit in your car: women with spiked heels; women with high hairdos; Cher; Scarlett O'Hara; Cleopatra; Las Vegas showgirls; a six-foot-tall all-girl-rock-band drummer with a Mohawk haircut. You know the type.

If you luck out and do get a date, swallow your pride. Take her to see *Flashdance* or *Stayin' Alive*. Go see that French movie. And if she comes to your apartment for that Amaretto nightcap, keep a copy of *Ms.* or *Mother Jones* on your coffee table. If you don't have a coffee table, rent one. Women love a man with a coffee table.

Finally, if a woman seems interested in you, for whatever reason, ignore my previous advice. Go out with her for God's sake. If you're anything like me, and I hope you're not, you gotta take what you get.

In a fern bar, 9/19/83

Herpes

Herpes. The Love Bug. The *Time-Life* empire says it's an epidemic. I could have told you that. We didn't need that picture on the cover of *Time:* anxiety-ridden young people standing in front of a hopeless wall, with the word Herpes scrawled in bright-red letters, letters as bright as Jayne Mansfield's mouth and twice as scary, sort of helter-skelter lettering, doomsday lettering. And what does *Time* call herpes? "The New Scarlet Letter," a reference to the famous novel by Nathaniel Hawthorne, a better writer than the staff of *Time* and a man who, I'm sure, did not have herpes. Who does have herpes? We know who has herpes.

Respectable young people, people on the go, guys and gals who jog, who ride ten-speed bicycles, upwardly mobile, tanned and healthy people. The sexual rebels of the '60s, slim and trim, they drink Lo-Cal beer, diet wine; they wear those little alligators on the left side of the shirt. Herpes is the lie of that perfect society: graffiti on a clean white wall, the mark of Cain, the blot on the escutcheon (whatever that means), a mistake.

That's right, guys and gals, a six-pack and a date on a country road won't get you babies anymore, and no shot-gun wedding, just occasional blisters. That's why I don't jog. What's the sense in meeting people? And what's the sense in eating vitamins and starch blockers and kelp and spirulina, any of that dried-out green stuff sold by forty-year-old hippies with gnats flying around their dreamy eyes. Herpes is the worm in the high-tech apple, you Cosmo gals and Playboys. But who's eating the apple? Who's minding the store? *Time* Magazine.

Herpes is the synthesis of some bizarre dialectic, proof that the Russians are right. Do Russians have herpes? Does the PLO have herpes? Or Americans who have been faithfully married for fifteen years and live in a three-bedroom split-level in Larchmont, or some exurbia that was *nice* in the '50s before the bad elements moved in? Now the shattered families are lonely in their ranch-style homes. The family's breaking down. The only decent thing on television is *Hill Street Blues*, and that's boring. Television is boring. The family is boring. The family is afraid. But the family doesn't have herpes. The kids who left home have herpes. The typical *Time-Life* reader is the one with herpes.

Time Magazine gives you its version of the world and puts you there, but it's not the world *I* live in. The *Time-Life* world is this strange alternative universe, a looking-glass world where everything has the same flat look—murder and movies, people and politics all get the same slightly snide even-handed style. To the average reader the threat of nuclear annihilation, the "situation" in the Mideast, the flights to outer space—all get the same weight in the Luce empire prose as photo captions of Marilyn Monroe, who seems to pop up in *Life* Magazine every five years or so, like some kind of periodic half-clad goddess. Marilyn Monroe's image seems to have the same kind of significance to the people at *Life* as images of the Virgin in small south-of-the-border villages. All right, I'm bitter. I applied for a job at *Time* reviewing records, and they wouldn't hire me. But history has shown me the world is full of tragedy, revenge, larger-than-life events; how does that tragedy compare with the embarrassment and inconvenience of herpes? Herpes might be irritating, but people aren't going to start bringing wet suits and gloves to intimate contact with other human beings.

They might stop reading *Time* Magazine though. I would. Look where you buy that thing—at newsstands. Thousands of people have thumbed through those magazines. Who knows what diseases those readers have. You don't know where *Time* has been, you only know where it's coming from, because I just told you.

In the library, 4/10/82

The Equal Rights Amendment

The Equal Rights Amendment is dead. Let me tell you why. From "Stupid Girl" to "Bad Girl," "This Girl" to *That Girl*, the rocky road of pop culture has been sprinkled with broken hearts and teenage love. While your famous pop crooner can cry all the way to the bank, the feminists have been crying to another tune and the lyrics are angrier than anything young Bob Dylan ever could have dreamed. Here's the bottom line, America: feminism has never had a Top Forty hit. Woody Allen has hits: about wimpy men and neurotic women, the kind of people who support ERA, the kind of people who call movies films. Artists and editors, nervous New Yorkers, Kramer versus Kramer's, highly educated people who stay away from the World of Dinettes and Stools, the world of Formica, the world of Tammy Wynette. My mother's world.

My mother saw Gloria Steinem on Phil Donahue, so she didn't go for the ERA. But what does Mother know? The last movie she saw was *Godfather II* and the last record she bought was *Pop Goes the Bach* by the Swinging Freshmen. She doesn't even watch *Rockford Files*, she watches Lawrence Welk. It's this whole fifties Perry Mason mentality. Della Street dialing the phone with a pencil. Women today have push-button phones, women today use their fingers. Today even Phyllis Schlafly takes her gloves off when she makes a phone call. That's high-tech telecommunication equality that the law can't touch.

Say it's the worst of all possible worlds and I get married like my mother wants. Oh yeah, I really want a wife wearing high heels and a garter belt and those pouty *Penthouse* lips greeting me when I get home from my nonsense job selling real estate or insurance to some desperate lower-middle-class family. I really want some goofy airhead bringing me my briefcase wearing nothing but perfume, nothing on but the radio, bringing me a pitcher of martinis, calling me Honey, jabbering about the Communist threat and the unraveling fabric of the American family. And kids. I really want kids when I'm cruising the strip checking out the hot new bands.

My mother sniffs at me and says I look like a girl. Hey Mom I'm thirty years old, okay? My girlfriend doesn't think I look like a girl, but then she doesn't look like a girl either. But what does it matter? We're equal. When we go out for fries at 3 A.M. after the bars close, she pays for hers and I pay for mine. Then I go home alone to my furnished room. There's Brooke Shields on the all-night movie looking like some Pre-Raphaelite Madonna. She's writhing on the floor, she says "Nothing comes between me and my Calvins." Nobody wants to come between her and her Calvins. Least of all me. That's what entropy is all about. We all get what we want in America, but what we want is so boring.

After a bad date, 5/3/81

Abortion

In the days when philosophers contemplated the nature of the universe, philosophers were a force in society. We don't have philosophers anymore, we have spokesmen, experts and commentators. We don't get poisoned like Socrates or tortured by the Inquisition. We can say whatever we want to, we just keep on talking until, like old soldiers, issues and experts fade away or dissolve into tomorrow's controversy.

In this context, abortion is a false debate, full of sound and fury, empty rages and empty love, and carefully staged around the headlines, pro on the left and con on the right. The vast confused middle of America just goes about its business, making decisions as best it can.

I don't want to drop more bitter words into the salt of this emotional ocean. After all, I've never had an abortion, but I will say I don't think abortion is a kind of liberal hobby, like patchwork quilts or knitting, the way Pro Lifers seem to think.

And I will say this: near as I can tell, the typical Pro Life person is a housewife who feels, with some justification, that feminism views her as some kind of alien creature just because she wants to stay home and raise a family. A housewife sees feminism as a condescending movement that places self above family, and devotes more attention to the origins of orgasms than the origins of life.

Pro Lifers feel like they're being talked down to. They've been made to feel that they did not choose to be housewives, but were somehow brainwashed into it. If she had a real choice, a housewife would be a graphic artist, a book editor, a psychologist, or at the very least, Erma Bombeck.

Pro Life says it's murder, Pro Choice says it doesn't matter, but they're just squeaky wheels making noise at each other. Perhaps if they talked to each other instead of to an issue, they'd find more in common.

Because the fact of the matter is, many people in the world don't have a choice in how, or even if, they live their lives. We are not a nation where people die in droves, where dissenters go up in smoke. Like a good little commentator, I'll continue to venture strong opinions on issues that will never touch my life, but in this pampered nation where Cabbage Patch dolls get more love and attention than human beings, it's hard for me to take a debate on abortion seriously.

Tired of the arguments, 1/29/85

Playboy

The Playboy Foundation wants to donate money to the MS. Foundation for Women. This seems like a peace offering at first blush, but if you think about it, *Playboy* giving money to a reproductive rights program is the ultimate in the Playboy philosophy. It's like mailing a check to your girlfriend instead of driving her to the clinic and pacing in the waiting room. *MS.* refused the money. They say it's because *Playboy* is sexist, but I think it's really because *Playboy* didn't act like a gentleman.

Playboy's image is getting a little threadbare around the cummerbund. In the 1950s *Playboy* opened the door to foolish male sexuality. In the 1960s a zillion other men's magazines jumped through that door, redecorated the den, and slammed the door in *Playboy*'s face. *Playboy* likes to think it appeals to men who like to think they're hip and attractive, but hip and attractive men don't spend their free time gawking at gauzy pictures of naked women. Hip and attractive men gawk at gauzy pictures of men's clothing and stereo component systems.

Playboy gives us the squarest of music tips, excerpts from the most boring best-sellers, stupid cartoons, and tips on the new electronics that are roughly six months out of date. *Playboy*'s lost the edge.

Those of us who used to sneak peeks at *Playboy* to see women with no clothes on, have gone on to men's magazines with a less complicated image. Nobody desires the playmate anymore—that innocent girl next door who has dreamed all her life of posing without a stitch, the way some women dream of becoming astronauts and physicists. *Playboy*'s light is shrinking, like a small boy in a man's tuxedo.

Because among all the gadgets, the fancy clothes, the full-color illustrations, among all the playmates, the playboy himself is disappearing. Pia Zadora is more than a match for a playboy. The women who read *MS.* or *Cosmo* are more than a match for the playboy. And if a playboy can't handle his playmates, if the world has passed the playboy by, it's a lonely bachelor's life in the bachelor's pad. The playboy must swing alone, dancing the two-step in his silk kimono, shuffling along his shag carpeting, trying to find the beat in that battered Brubeck platter.

I don't think *Playboy* and *Cosmopolitan* are evil. They don't cause crime rates to rise, they only feed the self-delusions of men and women with too much leisure time. And if *Playboy* wants to give money to feminist causes, they're probably dumb to give it, but it's even dumber not to take it. Don't get angry or offended with *Playboy*. A quick snort of contempt or a sneer of dismissal will do, then take the money and laugh all the way to the bank.

At the newsstand, 10/5/83

Single in the '80s

The word Yuppie doesn't connote a Gary Hart supporter to me, but rather conjures the image of a tiny aquarium fish with perhaps a small amount of brain damage. No wonder Yuppies have trouble getting dates. None of us Yuppies seems to have friends anymore, or knows how to use the telephone. Instead, we're going to the Personals columns or computer dating services, bringing the same kind of fleshless efficiency to our private lives that we bring to our work. Well, this is one Yuppie who still prefers flirtation and romance to relationships.

In the section of the daily paper called Life/Style there used to be handy guides to the opposite sex, usually with a title like "Is there lunch after marriage?" or "Refrigerators of the Stars." There used to be articles about wine, chocolate and orgasms, but all that has fallen by the wayside.

The swinging singles are all laid low with herpes. The peculiar joyless enthusiasm that feminists brought to their bodies in the '70s, and the smirking headwagging that *Time* Magazine brought to the bedroom, all of that strange stew we called the Sexual Revolution has been thrown out the window to be replaced by caution. Caution, pals and gals, is not an aphrodisiac.

Americans seem to need books to tell them what sexuality is supposed to be, and I guess I'm just as American as the next gazebo. I read *Cosmo* and *Ms.* to find the flip sides of what the gals are and aren't up to, I tried to generate a male lifestyle through cover-to-cover reading of *Esquire* and *Rolling Stone*.

But now we're supposed to be part of the New Celibacy, as advocated by Germaine Greer, who seems to have turned into a kind of feminist Ann Landers, urging young girls to save themselves for kids and marriage.

Granted, the sexual revolution went too far, information-wise. When you find phrases like "suck face" as a euphemism for "kiss" it sort of takes the zing out of intimate personal contact. And I really don't want to know the precise location of a lover's fallopian tubes. I don't want to be an Ob/Gyn, I just want a simple steamy workout in the dead of night.

Did I learn all my conversation gambits for nothing? Am I supposed to fall back on *serious* conversation? Give me a break. I boned up on astrology. I learned how to play Trivial Pursuit, for God's sake. I even shelled out hard-earned money for a French movie or two. It's embarrassing enough having all this garbage in my head, but now I'm not even going to be rewarded for it? I say put the New Celibacy on the back burner, at least while I'm around.

If I wanna be repressed I'll learn how to fix cars, smoke cigars, play poker, and buy a personal computer. Male bonding is highly overrated, let me tell you, and it will never be as much fun as sex.

Between calls, 5/12/84

Weddings

I just broke up with what was, by my count, my twenty-third girlfriend. I was low on money, down in spirits, and down on my luck when—in the debris she left behind—I found a wedding invitation.

She had known the couple, not me, but I RSVP'ed anyway, much to the chagrin of the bride and groom. I slept through the vows—I hate watching people make a public promise: if you can keep it you're bragging, and if you can't, why tell the world about it? At the reception, however, my stomach full of free food and cheap bar scotch, sitting at a table in the rear of the Howard Johnson's multipurpose room, a large table filled with undesirable relatives and me, I listened to the band and thought back on all the weddings I've seen through the years.

The Polish weddings, where the official drink was 7 & 7, and the only thing to eat was great hunks of bloody roast beef, where stiff-necked old couples danced with bodies as nimble as their faces were frozen; the Jewish wedding, where the glass was smashed under the heel; the hippie wedding, where red balloons flew up, and the dog bit the minister from the Universal Life Church; the Catholic wedding, where the best man had too much to drink and put grape Fizzies in the Holy Water.

In courtrooms, hotels, warehouses, parks, backyards, churches, under water, in the sky—vows and rings are exchanged, flowers are thrown, bulbs flash. We see the forced good humor of the father of the bride, who fingers his checkbook and hopes the liquor will last long enough for everybody to pass out or go home. We hear the airy platitudes of Kahlil Gibran or the stern sexism of Saint Paul, the tuxedoed musicians who can make the most bizarre musical transitions you can imagine—from Havah Nagilah to Maniac to Michael Jackson to Prince. They can play anything you request, but every tune will sound like a polka.

As I sat and listened to "I Wanna Be Sedated" by the Ramones (my request), I thought about romance. I remembered girlfriend number three. Like all teenage boys in the '60s, I played the guitar, and like all teenage girls, girlfriend number three had a voice as sweet as Joni Mitchell's. We were invited to a friend's wedding to sing "Bridge Over Troubled Water" and "White Bird." I expected a little money out of the deal—after all, I'd learned two new chords—but the only payment I got was an English Leather grooming set, even though I had a struggling beard at the time and the only soap I used was Dr. Bronner's.

Like the saps we were, girlfriend three and I got high on cheap champagne and made our own wedding plans. A month later of course, she ran off with a bass player named Rocky, I traded my guitar for a battered Underwood typewriter that couldn't make capital letters, and I started on my long career of cultural commentary.

So. Twenty girlfriends later, I watched two families join and dance, watched the dark groom and pale bride kissing under the spinning lights, and I thought of those scary words, "Till Death Do Us Part," and all the weddings ripped by divorce.

Maybe the true wedding dance is done by lawyers to the rhythms of prenuptial agreements, and maybe I'm just married to irony, but I know that love is more than a score in a tennis game. I might be a curmudgeon, but I miss that old guitar and the battered Underwood. I even miss girlfriend three. When my mother told me girlfriend three had married a real-estate salesman and moved to Ohio, my cold heart jumped a bit, sure. But to tell you the truth, today I can't remember her name.

On the road, June '84

A History of the Moon

I ducked out of the pouring rain today into a porno theater. I plopped down next to a man in an orange suit, who was carrying three plastic shopping bags. His inward mumbles were louder than the sound track. Not that a porno sound track was something I wanted to slap on the old turntable but still, I'd paid my five bucks, it was part of the package.

Midway through the disjointed close-ups, terrible jokes about body parts, and inappropriate music, amid all the erasures of the mysteries of the flesh, the filmmakers cut away from pink skin to a shot of a full moon through an open window. Immediately I remembered where I was—in a porno theater next to some welfare case with left-brain/right-brain chemistry askew, the rain tapping on the roof, among coughing lonely men. The full moon filled the screen for five full seconds before we got back to the action, as they say. So now that's part of the history of the moon.

In my fourth-grade spelling period we divided the class up into Russia and America, each with its own rocket. With each correct spelling, each group moved closer to the moon that we had chalked on the blackboard. In fourth grade as in life, America got there first. That's the history of the moon.

Parked in a '65 Ford in the autumn of '67, I saw the moon like a diamond on the flowing river. We drove to the drive-in, and I chased my girlfriend barefoot through the lines of parked cars, lit by a werewolf's head in some British horror flick, lit by the light of the real full moon, chasing her through the woods and into the poison ivy. I itched for two weeks and she never saw me again. The history of the moon.

I remember the astronauts in *Life* Magazine, posing in the vacuum with the flag frozen in midwave. The empty craters of the moon were reflected in the mirrors they had for faces. Shadows on a dead face. The history of the moon.

This dead rock in the sky pulls on the vast oceans of the earth, pulls on the psyches of lunatics and lovers. The first kiss, the first wine, under the bridge, the full moon over the trees.

I walked out of the porno theater into the driving rain. There wasn't a moon to be seen in the sky, but I had a phone call to make. I made the call. She hung up on me. The history of the moon.

Downtown, 11/12/82

THE ARTS

Humanism

There's been a lot of talk over the past ten years or so about that mysterious slippery thing called "secular humanism." *Humanist*, as you all know, is both a badge worn proudly by liberals, and a contemptuous epithet thrown at liberals by the religious right. Humanism, according to the right, is responsible for all kinds of evil—the collapse of family, education and religion, as well as the rise of homosexuality and rock and roll. Well, don't worry, America, humanism doesn't stand a chance.

Humanism doesn't have any *stories*. Humanists are boring. Contrast a humanist magazine like *Saturday Review* with its opposite, *Reader's Digest*. Which do you read at the dentist's office? Contrast Nicholas Von Hoffmann with Paul Harvey. Who would *you* rather listen to? We've got a President now who can whip through Bartlett's *Familiar Quotations* to find an appropriate homily for *whatever* crisis rears its ugly head. What would we have had with Walter Mondale?

I don't know what the traditional American values *are*, exactly, but I sure know those stories by heart—George Washington couldn't tell a lie, so he threw a silver dollar across the Potomac and crossed the Delaware, the Little Engine that could, and God liked the gift of the Littlest Angel the best of all, Abe Lincoln split a rail and freed the slaves, the brave boys died at the Alamo, the brave boys died with Custer, Diogenes searched the world with his lantern for an honest man, Roosevelt wore glasses and charged up San Juan Hill when he got the message from Garcia. Remember the Man Without a Country? Goofus and Gallant? The Boston Tea Party?

Remember *these* voices:

> Shoot if you will this old gray head, but spare my
> country's flag; I have not yet begun to fight; I regret
> that I have but one life to give for my country; 'tis a
> far far better thing I do; you may fire when ready
> Gridley; No Taxation without Representation;
> 54-40 or fight; Retreat, Hell! Surrender, Nuts!;
> Carry me over the river boys and let me rest under
> the trees; breathes there a man with soul so dead
> who never to himself hath said; he who steals my
> purse steals trash; say it ain't so Joe; and ask not
> what your country can do for you?

We got the highway man who's riding, the young man who
stood on the burning deck, the captain, brave captain, the cats
and dogs and Boy Scouts who pull small children from burning buildings, and the little drummer boy *ba rum ba bum bum*.

All of us have this colorful mush stuck in our heads as the
result of twelve years of public education. But contrast this
trite sentimentality with humanism. Jean-Paul Sartre? His
turgid prose defeats his own philosophy. If the world is meaningless, why would despair have any more meaning than joy? I
mean I'm as existential as the next guy, but I prefer Bogart,
Bugs Bunny, and the Marx Brothers as role models, or the Cat
in the Hat, before he became an educational tool.

Of course the ultimate humanist book is *1984*, which
everybody has read but *nobody* likes. And I guess the ultimate
humanist actor is John Hurt, star of the latest movie version of
1984. I don't know about the rest of you, but I think John
Hurt should lighten up. Somebody give the guy a comedy,
quick. I'm tired of watching that poor sap suffer.

On Memory Lane, 2/15/85

115

The State of the Arts

Yesterday's avant-garde becomes today's mainstream. Even dada and surrealism have a heritage. So when I read that Salvador Dali was selling his signature on blank pieces of paper, I wondered: Is Dali trying to make a buck by endorsing his own forgeries? Is he creating a conceptual art piece? These thoughts flew through my mind briefly before I said, "Who cares?" To my mind the only great artists of the twentieth century are Norman Rockwell and Pablo Picasso. Mondrian gives me a headache, Jackson Pollack is inaccessible and ugly. Op art makes my eyes hurt. Hyperrealism was just glorified paint-by-number, and pop art had too fine an irony, depending on Andy Warhol's vision of American culture, and I have no interest in Andy Warhol's vision of anything. We have to go back to the Middle Ages to find a pure artistic vision.

What's our glory now? Half-deep aesthetics that are more important than the works the aesthetic produces. Conceptual art—collections of washrags from gas stations in Nevada, collages of garbage from the side of the freeway. These art "pieces"—they're always called pieces—are created from a combination of contempt for the viewing public and flattery for the Philistines that hand out the grants. Broken pieces of glass and paint chips are presented at museums with a straight face. Video presentations of skinny naked women superimposed over toasters and atomic bombs. When are people going to learn that the only things television is good for are rock videos, game shows, news and soap operas. There is no such thing as "video art."

Take a look at schlock art—paintings on velvet, fuzzy puppies, happy clowns. These paintings may be vulgar, but at least there's an honest relationship between painter and viewer. Average Joe gives the painter at his parking-lot stand fifty bucks. The painter got paid, and Average Joe's got a seascape with gulls that matches his rattan sectional perfectly. Painter and buyer both know what they're getting.

So what is "art"? Art is a grant proposal. The artist describes his piece to the foundation. Let's say it's a "video poem on time's artifacts in the physical world." The foundation takes a meeting, then fires off a couple of thou to the video artist, who spends a weekend doing a five-hour video close-up of waxed fruit (with synthesizer music) and a monotone voice-over in French, then blows the rest of the money on cheap red jug wine, so he can argue with his friends about whether Imagism is decadent or not. Who cares? Nobody cares about art anymore, unless it's an album cover, a magazine spread, or the back of a cereal box. Art is just window dressing for products, and it's time we stopped pretending otherwise. Turn the museums into dance halls or low-income housing. Give the paintings to the poor, give the grant money to me. Art is dead. Kiss it good-bye.

At the museum, 5/26/83

Doonesbury

My big gripe with the world today is there's too much information about the world, and not enough information about me. News is fine—don't get me wrong—I want to know how much makeup President Reagan wore on *Death Valley Days* as much as the next American. I like to lie back of an evening and try to figure out just what word that rhymes with *rich* Mrs. Bush meant. Paying attention to the news makes me feel like a citizen, all right, but it's not going to make me any money. The only way to make money from the news is to be part of it.

I want to be quoted in the headlines. I want my picture on the front page, I want to be photographed by contest winners as I walk briskly from my limo to my private jet. I want to be surrounded by stern-looking men with reflector shades and snub-nosed Israeli machine guns hidden under their three-piece suits. I want to pick out reporters with a firm jab of the finger and give hard answers to hard questions. I want to tie up traffic for a twenty-mile radius, for no good reason.

No, I don't want to be President, or even a Presidential hopeful. I just want to be a media figure. I just want to talk to the press. And I'm ready.

Ian Shoales as news. It's an exciting new concept, but it's a bandwagon nobody seems willing to jump on. I'm used to being ignored, but the straw that broke the camel's back, me being the camel, was the return of Doonesbury. Why the return of Doonesbury was news, I don't know. I have to admit I didn't feel even the vaguest sense of loss when Doonesbury left, and I can't really say my life is fuller now that it's back, but I can say I'm mighty disappointed that Garry Trudeau missed the boat. He could have included me in the Doonesbury pantheon of characters.

He did it for Hunter Thompson, why not do it for me? I already look like everybody else in Doonesbury—painfully thin, dark circles under the eyes, slightly stoop-shouldered. I realize my acid tongue might make mincemeat of his other characters, but I think he could capture the essential me if he really tried—my great sorrows, my vast rages, my sage opinions, the laughter, the tears. Well, he wouldn't have to worry about the tears. I haven't cried since Old Yeller died.

Better act fast, Garry, I've got other fish on the line. I've already offered to be a hydrophobic dog for Garfield, a corrupt purchase officer for Beetle Bailey, a real Viking to show Hägär the Horrible how it's done (you know, the kind of Viking who drinks mead from human skulls); I've offered to be Doonesbury for Bloom County, I've offered to marry Fritzi Ritz, or be Mr. Goodbar for Cathy. Gimme a break, Garry, I wanna be newsworthy. If you don't help me out, I might have to run for public office or even worse, go to work for a living. Call my agent soonest. My image is available, for sale or rent.

Reading the paper, 10/25/84

Censors

According to the self-appointed watchdogs of our culture, *Huckleberry Finn* is too racist for the young to read, *The Color Purple* too violent. Kids today can't have prayer in schools, fairy tales, evolution, or breakdancing at the mall. Even Disney cartoons are under attack. And now we have the new PG-13 rating—more numbers and codes designed to do the parents' job for them. I know the price of freedom is eternal vigilance, but can't the vigilantes take a break once in a while? Right-wingers like to brag that this is the greatest country on earth, yet they think their own children are potential psychopaths who need only the spark of bad pop culture to set them on a rampage. Vigilantes on the left, on the other hand, worry about books and movies creating a "climate of violence," "desensitizing" our children. This concern for the sensitivity of the young is touching, but don't the critics realize the very elements they object to are the same elements kids think are the "cool parts"?

What's at stake here, you see, is America's moral fiber. Moral fiber is a mysterious substance strong enough to make America great, but flimsy enough to unravel at the merest hint of undue excitement. Critics think that American youth is a fragile boat rocking in a pitiless sea of immorality. One little tip and the kids will either drown in a sea of evil or grow up to be hit men.

All of this leads me to hate parents—not mine, of course, but the principle of the thing. Parents are okay when they stay at home, but when they start messing with what America can do and see, they're trouble and a discipline problem to boot. I've got nothing against burning books—I've burned the latest by Norman Mailer and Joan Didion myself: it keeps me warm on a cold night and makes me think my opinion has an impact; but I've got my own fireplace and my own matches. Don't keep books and movies out of my grasp just because you're afraid they'll give your precious one nightmares.

And what do we want books and movies to be about anyway? Puppy dogs and kitty cats? Smurfs and bunny rabbits? Sure, pop culture gives us inane fantasies based on our deepest fears and desires, but remember, bitterness, lust and greed are the stuff of art as well as dreck. Go ahead and number and code the culture, and you'll get exactly what you want: a culture as sensitive and moral as all get out, smarmy best sellers and bland blockbusters with no cool parts at all.

On the couch, 6/30/84

Theater Today

If the American theater isn't dead, maybe we should put the poor thing out of its misery. I know, I know, New Yorkers will say what do you know about theater on the West Coast anyway? And you're right—the stages out here that are not closed down because of fire-code violations, union problems, lack of parking, and lack of money are usually filled with what is called "performance art." Performance art is created by thin young men and usually consists of dancerly women taking their clothes off, putting on masks, and dumping blood on each other while a sound track screeches out machinery noises. You can sneer at this, New Yorkers, but the *Village Voice* loves these things as much as your Californian, especially if it's performance art from Czechoslovakia, or has music by Philip Glass. I'll admit freely, my theater criticism comes from the Ian Shoales sour-grapes principle. Ever since I made my fifth-grade entrance as a large shoe, in the Lewis and Clark Grade School production of *Shoemaker and the Elves*, I've had the greasepaint roaring in my heated veins, but have agents scraped their knuckles on my door? No. I'm following my own advice. If they don't let you do it, sneer at them. It's a poor ethic, but mine own.

Sure, I haven't been to Broadway since 1975, and the only things I saw then were a smug and silly Tom Stoppard play, self-consciously written and staged, in which the actors arched their eyebrows so intensely I thought they were going to get neck sprain, and a production of *Hamlet* in which the lead actor shouted every line in a voice that sounded exactly like Dudley Do Right, I'll admit that. But not seeing something has never stopped me from having an opinion before. Besides, I read the *Times*. My big gripe with the *New York Times* is the lack of a comics page, but it still keeps me up to date on what's squirming in the Big Apple.

And you don't have to be a critic to wonder why any sensible person would go to New York, then shell out fifty-plus bucks to see a play about cats, a musical about cats, a musical about cats based on light verse by T.S. Eliot. If ever a poet was less capable of a playful mood than T.S., a name doesn't spring to mind. Or go see a musical about drag queens. I've got nothing against drag queens, but I can see them on the street for free. And what about *Sunday in the Park with George*? A Stephen Sondheim musical about neo-Impressionism? Hold me back.

You can keep Tom Stoppard's latest; and the two Davids, Mamet and Rabe, might be excoriating, powerful and hard-hitting, like the critics say, but I happen not to like excoriating powerful and hard-hitting experiences. I wouldn't mind seeing Whoopi Goldberg, if only because John Simon dismissed her in that snide prose style it's taken him a lifetime to master, but I'll wait till she comes home to California and save a few bucks.

Why are we importing all these highbrow plays like *Amadeus*? I could've told you Mozart was a jerk for nothing. And his music sounds like the sound track to movies I don't want to see. I hate it. I hate opera, all those unnatural voices shouting about vanished passions in a language I don't understand. Why don't we look to the theater around us—sports, high-school graduation ceremonies, politics? All these things are theater, but this aesthetic of watching culture not because you like it, but so you can pat yourself on the back for seeing it, that's not theater, that's Victorian nonsense; theater today is either Broadway or grant-proposal gibberish.

Theater today has no life, no art; and nobody's paying attention except a handful of rich theatergoers, who have been blackmailed into appreciation by a smaller handful of critical snobs. Theater today is pop culture for the rich, created either by the self-indulgent, hacks, or the British. I might be going out on a limb with that statement, but go ahead and saw it off. I don't mind falling. Might be a good publicity gimmick. Maybe a producer will notice.

On the couch, 12/17/84

Sick Jokes

Against my better judgment I went to see a movie everybody's talking about, *Stranger Than Paradise*. I thought it was an hour too long and looked like every French movie I saw twenty years ago, but the very American shaggy-dog, mildly sick twist at the end got me thinking about the nature of jokes. Many movies and books are just extended sick jokes. *Love Story* springs to mind, when Ryan O'Neal pushes aside the I.V. tubes to share a tender moment with Ali McGraw. I remember vividly that the scene in *Valley of the Dolls* in which Patty Duke tries to sing a duet with a brain-damaged pop singer had me screaming so hysterically I had to be escorted to the lobby by two burly ushers and forbidden to see a movie in that theater again unless I signed a written statement that I would control my emotions. Of course that was merely bad taste, but even a great work of art like *Lolita* is a sick joke, and Americans love sick jokes.

You know what I'm talking about. The joke you heard by the photocopy machine about Vanessa Williams? The joke about Claudine Longet that had you groaning in your coffee? Mommy mommy jokes, little-Willy jokes, Idi Amin jokes, Hitler-and-Holocaust jokes, jokes about Ethiopia, famine, disease, plague, death, the suffering of innocent people, Anne Frank jokes, Helen Keller jokes. You've heard them. You've told them.

When I was a boy we played a boys' game called "Which Would Be Worse?" "Would you rather be blind or deaf? Would you rather lose an arm or a leg? Would you rather be staked on the ground and have bamboo grow through you or staked on a beach in a swarm of hungry crabs? Would you rather have bamboo splints put under your fingernails or be rolled down a hill in a barrel full of nails?"

Of course, the "Which Would Be Worse?" game was the direct result of too many James Bond novels, but it goes to show that the human heart has many chambers and the world *is* a cruel place. Maybe the sick joke isn't so much a cynical response to cruel events, as a frightened response to our own knowledge of these events. The sick joke posits a world even worse than the one we live in, and if we can laugh at that, or even just say, "Eeyew," and go back to work, well maybe there's no harm in it, so long as we keep the moral juices flowing and the CARE packages in the mail.

Despite the fact that we shell out hard-earned money to gawk at pictures of dead movie stars in a book like *Hollywood Babylon*, or use pictures of fetuses, bludgeoned baby seals, or starving children to bolster respective ideologies in the same way an advertiser uses copy points to push a product, I still hope moral outrage is a pure emotional condition, and not the creepy residue of disturbing images displayed for our consumption.

But I have to admit I don't like sick jokes much, and if they are a problem, I've got a solution—the bland joke. The bland joke is designed to replace the ethnic joke, the sick joke, the joke of reduction. If the Lutherans don't mind, I thought I'd make them the subject of a series of jokes. Try these around the water cooler:

> Why did the Lutheran cross the road?
> To check with his insurance agent about automobile coverage.

> How many Lutherans does it take to screw in a light bulb?
> One.

123

How many Lutherans can fit in a Volkswagen?
Four comfortably. Five, if one is a child.

You get the idea. I think they're inoffensive, but if any Lutherans object, how about a bland limerick?

> I went to the movies and then
> I took the bus homeward again.
>   I took a short nap
>   With my hands in my lap,
> And got off at my stop around ten.

Come on, let's get that oral tradition back on its feet. I've got the ball rolling, now it's up to you. Which would be worse? Would you rather be mildly amused by a bland joke or say "Eeyew" so hard you spill hot coffee all over yourself? The choice, America, is yours.

Not laughing, 2/16/85

MUSIC

Rock Music Today

A while back I noticed advertisements for a new video game featuring the pop group Journey. This seemed to be the logical extension of the jukebox and MTV. What Journey does is almost like music, and their video game should have been almost like fun. The video game went bust, but Journey goes on.

Rock has never been music, really. It was just noise. It used to be shouting and banging in garages. We used to think, I could sing like that, and we were right. Even the Beatles started out as a bunch of goofball kids, until money changed them. Lawyers, accountants, agents, managers, roadies, T-shirt makers, demographics, drugs and ambition have changed rock forever.

And now that books and movies aren't any good anymore, critics are going after rock music with a vengeance. It's strange to see the old critical buzz words like *stunning* and *powerful*—adjectives once found exclusively in book reviews—taken away from Jerzy Kosinski and given to some drug-addict guitar player.

Rockers used to belong to the special world of Bad Celebrities, people like Errol Flynn and Joan Crawford, or Katherine Crosby when she sold Bing's golf clubs (that's like selling a piece of the true cross). Lady Di might yet become a Bad Celebrity. She might snap in the limelight, buy a handgun, and pop off some *paparazzi*.

But rockers are Good Celebrities now. As Mick Jagger moves into his forties, his clothes get nicer, we see him eating in gourmet restaurants (and ordering in French). Soon he'll have a U.S. Open named after him, and he'll start playing tennis with Alan Alda.

All the Bad Boys are gone, and the slow-talking platter pushers in the dead of night. The ghosts of rock and roll used to haunt us as we drove. But that's rock-and-roll history and it's over. The Beatles killed it.

Rock music used to be about dancing and parties, stolen kisses and fast cars. Then, in the late '60s, the Beatles pretended to be Sergeant Pepper's Lonely Hearts Club Band. The producer overorchestrated every track, the critics dubbed it a *concept* album and the beginning of the end had begun.

> *Tommy: A Rock Opera;* four sides about a deaf, mute and blind kid who plays pinball and becomes a Messiah. If this had been a novel, it would have been laughed off the page.
>
> *Aqualung;* four sides about an old wino with tuberculosis. Wanna dance?

Concepts are to albums what plots are to hack novelists. From the incredibly silly *The Beat Goes On* by the Vanilla Fudge to the sublime *Good Old Boys* by Randy Newman or magnificent *Nightfly* by Donald Fagen—everybody and the family dog have made one, and that trend too has come to an end.

Now it's all rock history and what we have today are just comments on that history. Stray Cats try to sound like Carl Perkins, The Clash come on like pseudo-socialist Rolling Stones, and U2 comes on like The Clash. Devo has run its obvious joke into the dialectical ground. Men At Work sound like The Police, and The Police sound like blond Jamaicans. Springsteen was hailed as the new Dylan, and now John Cougar wants to be the new Springsteen. The Beatles pretended to be Sergeant Pepper's Band for one album, now a group pretends to be someone else for a whole career.

This is fine if you're looking for irony and comments on a common history; it's not fine if you want to dance. You can't dance to irony. I want The Ramones—loud stupid songs about girlfriends and surfing. If I'm in a quieter mood, give me a stupid folk song about dogs. If I want stupid ideas I'll go back to college. Shut up, play the guitar, and keep your concepts to yourself.

At the record store, 6/15/83

Androgynes and Other Strangers

All the conspiracy seekers among us, both Falwellian and Orwellian, have been exercising their tongue muscles clucking at the concept of androgyny, which is supposed to be a *problem* for somebody. Androgynes are objects of terror, I guess, for those who seek to be terrified by pop-culture icons. Boy George, Prince, and Michael Jackson are usually held up as the quintessence of androgyny. But George was thoughtful enough to put a *boy* in front of his name; it's "Prince" not "Princ*ess*," and as for Michael Jackson, well, maybe there is such a thing as an androgynous Jehovah's Witness, but if there is, none has ever come to my door. So what's everybody so worried about? You gonna take a shower with these guys or listen to their music?

It seems to me the only problem an androgyne faces is what to do on a date. There's supposed to be something vaguely sensual about an androgyne, though frankly I don't know what you'd do with one if you had one—go to an Andy Warhol party, I guess, or start a band. If Prince and Nastassia Kinski start dating, for example, what would they do? Shop for clothes? What people mean when they say *androgynous* is really "rich" or "French" or "skinny."

On the meat of pop-culture unisex is just another tenderizer, a preservative to increase the shelf life of stars. It really doesn't mean anything. Male and female characteristics just aren't that easy to define. As a matter of fact, I'm not even sure that male and female exist anymore, except in perfume commercials.

Clint Eastwood, for example, is held up as a manly man. In

his last *Dirty Harry* movie, he decked a lesbian with one punch. Well sure, she hit him first, but what a woman—or a man for that matter—would find sexually attractive about this behavior is anybody's guess. And who am I, as an American man, supposed to find sexually appealing? Loni Anderson? Not for Ian. A man could fall into her coiffure and never be seen again.

If there is a moral to be gleaned from the sordid aftermath of the sexual revolution, it might be from Prince's movie *Purple Rain*. If you stop hitting your girlfriend you'll become a star. That is truly a message for our times. And here's my message: if you're over the age of, roughly, seventeen and feel a lack in your life of what is commonly called a "sexual role model," I recommend putting on side one of Prince's *1999* album. Bop till you drop, then take a brief nap. You'll feel a lot better, believe me.

In line for Prince tickets, February 8

Reggae Music

Reggae music comes from Jamaica. Reggae is the product of a poor oppressed society that ignores its own repression, calling their own island Babylon, with amused dismissal more than contempt, melancholy more than bitterness, displacing their own oppression with a vision of Africa as the Garden of Eden, the place they truly belong.

People like me hear reggae music and tell you about it. And more and more rich white Americans hear it, and bored L.A. musicians travel to Jamaica to cop that pure reggae sound, as slow as a hot swim, as sweet as magnolias. Reggae is one of the last sweet things left in the world, but nothing sweet ever gets left alone. Bitter British musicians caught reggae and turned it into anger. After all, broke British working-class kids don't even have Africa to look back to. They know what British history is. Just as porno movies make us long for the innocence of strippers, and video games make us long for pinball, reggae music makes us wish the world were a perfect place, a world where bad guys exist only so that heroes won't get bored.

I know parents don't like kids to listen to reggae music because it extols the so-called virtues of marijuana. Well, listen, *my* memories of marijuana are black lights and candles and racking coughs, and some long-haired jerk who'd turn the Moody Blues off, blow out the candles and ask some "mind-blowing" question like "What if everything small in the universe became large and everything large in the universe became small?" then turn *Ride My See Saw* up real loud and leave the room. Obnoxious, yes, but nothing for a loving mother to be afraid of. Comic books, movies, video games, drugs—listen, kids have to throw their quarters away on something. The only thing free in the world is sex. Believe me, kids today would much rather spend money than have sex, despite what Moral Majority or Planned Parenthood say. Give kids money. Money is simple. Sex, while fun, is complicated and has consequences. Consumerism has no consequences.

Everybody's so worried that something will have a bad moral effect on our young that we're hell-bent on removing all nightmares from our lives, so that we'll go the way we seem to be going—a prepackaged world of liberal and conservative consumers, with prepackaged opinions, leading lives of terminal jet lag, living in airports with quick phone calls between flights to assure everybody we're on the move, on the go, sneaking quick glances at *Time* and *Newsweek* to assure ourselves the world's still intact, quick glances at *The New Yorker* to assure ourselves we still have a culture. All our various camps of self-righteous frightened snobs think their Way Of Life is threatened, but a lifestyle struggle and a life-and-death struggle are two different things.

The real victims of the world stand in welfare lines, or crouch in the battle zone, under the jets, wishing *they* could have an opinion. They want to be rude. They want to talk with their mouths full. And they cling to the few genuine pleasures untouched by critics and parents, politicians and soldiers in this wretched world. Like comic books. Like action movies. Like physical pleasure. Like reggae music.

Listening to Bob Marley, 9/10/81

Overexposed

When the Jacksons put on their shades and plug in their amps this summer, they'll have to book entire states to contain the crowds, who will show Michael Jackson the kind of whole-hearted devotion usually reserved for Popes or a visitor from another planet. One could say that this kind of intense devotion to a frail young man verges on mass hysteria. Like the Kennedy clan, Elvis or John DeLorean, Michael Jackson is one of those media figures about whom we can never hear too much. We even devour stories about his *glove,* as if it were the magical totem of a saint. Understandably perhaps, Michael Jackson is the most nervous superstar we've ever had. If it's lonely at the top, like they say, *his* solitude is raised to a pitch not audible to the human ear. He hides in his room, afraid, say the stories. He rattles around in his limo with nothing to keep him company but old cartoons on the tape player. He's a monk, a hermit in the desert of fame.

We're meant to believe that the burden of the spotlight is almost too much for his fragile mortal frame to bear. He's supposed to be like some albino fish in a cave, drawn to the light but hurt by it, some beautiful shy creature that only comes alive in the spotlight, a creature who needs special clothing and sunglasses to keep from withering away. What we're supposed to feel for Michael Jackson, in other words, is not admiration, but pity. We're actually supposed to feel sorry for the guy!

Well, that much fame dropping on a person is almost pagan, and maybe we should stop paying attention before the poor guy cracks, like a doll of bone china clutched too hard by greedy grasping children. If he is, in effect, the twentieth-century equivalent of a human sacrifice, if he's suffering for our pleasure, let's remove the source of his pain. Maybe it's right that he should be overexposed at last, like a bubble-gum card dropped on the sidewalk to fade in the sun. Maybe we should turn the lights off for a while and give Michael Jackson a break. I'll put a rumor to rest now and get that ball rolling. In case you were wondering, I am the father of Billie Jean's child. It's off my chest at last, and I'm glad I said it here.

Experiencing pity and terror, 6/13/84

SPORTS

Baseball

I went to my first baseball game last week—the Giants against the Cardinals (or the *Cards*, as they're called in baseball lingo). Like most American pleasures, this one was mixed, half sleazy and half wholesome. America's artists and intellectuals have always had a fascination with this incredibly dull game, and sportswriters have always waxed poetic about it, in that unique prose you only find in your local sporting green. Teams never *win* in sports prose, they "squeeze out," or "edge out," or "rally," or "claw back." Sportswriters have to amuse themselves somehow at these boring games, and thinking up synonyms for "win" must help to while away those long hours.

All right, sure, if you're obsessed with numbers and statistics there's a limited appeal to baseball, and there is the lazy physical poetry of the men on the field, and the occult significance of the diamond, and it usually lasts only nine innings. But all this semi-enjoyment is offset mightily by the psychopathic behavior of the fans. Fistfights, booing, screaming, spilling beer, mindlessly responding to every command the scoreboard gives them: GO GO GO in letters eight feet tall with little animated cheerleaders to spur the home team on. The fans pour down gallons of overpriced beer, which the pitchmen pour two at a time (the athletics of the hawkers are much more energetic than those of the baseball players), and the end result is a bunch of screaming drunken bums who can barely stand up, but persist in trying, obstructing your view of the game, which may not be thrilling, but it's the only game around.

But I'd paid for my own ticket, I was going to enjoy myself

even if it killed me. I was sitting in Section 2 of Candlestick over the visitors' dugout, scribbling notes in my beer-soaked notebook. A foul ball came my way. I reached up and much to my surprise caught the thing, held on, and, I discovered later, broke my wrist in two places. So I got a souvenir, a firsthand glimpse of America's favorite pastime, and an insurance hike—all for six bucks.

Oh, the game. Bottom of the ninth, Bergman singled to center, bases loaded, LeMaster scoring. Giants took the game, edging the Cards five to four. Love that prose. Next week the cast comes off, and tomorrow? Tomorrow's another game.

On the couch, 5/27/83

Bad Sports

I avoid athletes like the plague unless they're in a Tarzan movie. I hate sports, having been the only child in America to receive a personal letter from the President's Council on Physical Fitness telling me I wasn't applying myself. To this day, I don't know what the President's Council on Physical Fitness did—lead Congress in the Jane Fonda Workout perhaps—but as a kid I imagined they had vague connections with the Secret Service, and unfitness was a form of disloyalty. Now, of course, I only stay in shape so I'll look good in designer clothing, but why are kids today being pushed so hard into sports?

Athletes stay in shape to go for the gold, and they get the gold so they can sell breakfast cereal. If Carl Lewis wants to plaster his face on a box of Sugar Whackies, that doesn't bother me. The guy has to make a buck. I'd put my face on Sugar Whackies myself if I could just convince an advertiser that sarcasm could really move a product—or that I was a role model for the young.

No, commercialism doesn't make people mad at Carl

Lewis, or John McEnroe, or Muhammad Ali. People got mad at Carl Lewis because he made it look too easy. Carl Lewis ruined the spectacle. We've seen too many movies and commercials where athletes push and strain, with close-ups of quivering thighs and slow-motion rivers of sweat. We want to see athletes *work* at it. We want them to be modest, clean-living, pure, and good losers. Well, we've never had good-loser jocks, and we never will. American athletes are the possessors of a product: the body.

Kids today are being pushed into athletics, not for the glory, but to make them little salespeople for their bodies. And sure, why not? I'm with you, kids. Get an agent, get a Porsche, write a screenplay. You could be the next Tarzan or Wonder Woman. You could be the model for next year's billboard, pitching running shoes to tomorrow's jocks, selling tomorrow's kids on the show business of sport. This will make you lots of money, and you won't have to work up a sweat doing it. Sports fans, if you want grunts, sweat, good and bad guys, watch professional wrestling. If you want sportsmanship, start your own team. And kids, if you're the type who gets chosen last for the baseball games, don't sweat it if you flunk the school fitness test. What are they gonna do? Keep your body back a year? Sit down, relax, watch a little TV. Why do you want to stay in shape anyway? You'll just grow up to be another fit consumer, with your body on a box.

Having breakfast, 8/25/84

Send in the Clowns

Certain individuals in this nation coughed up close to 1,200 bucks for lousy seats at the Super Bowl. Doesn't amaze me. Super Bowl is a spectacle. Even a normal football game is an event so epic you watch it on a television the size of a wall, and this was Super Bowl 19—or rather Super Bowl XIX. Now, that's worshipful. Roman numerals are usually reserved for world wars, or sequels to *Rocky*.

Face it, the Inauguration was upstaged. They had to wait till Monday to make it public. It was *Super Bowl* Sunday, not Inauguration Sunday, Inauguration 50, not L. Sure, the ceremony had the pomp and circumstance of power, trend-setting coiffures, Sinatra snarling at the media, Secret Service men with rocket launchers. But there was something missing.

I define a spectacle as a large harmless event that boggles the mind but leaves the heart alone—a parade, the circus, Ice Capades, the Olympics, those Las Vegas shows in which a hundred half-clad women stroll across a stage the size of a football field, on spiked heels, without wobbling. The Inaugural Committee's measly ten-million-dollar budget can't create a true spectacle. That kind of tackiness doesn't come cheap.

A true spectacle, like an Indian sand painting, always has a flaw. It's not Snoopy out there on the ice, it's a bored guy in a shopworn dog suit. The Vegas showgirl always has a glassy smile, the circus lion tamer always has a tattoo. Where were the tattoos at the Inauguration? There was no excitement.

At a football game, the crowd gets so excited they do the Wave: to my mind convincing evidence that a mob can be trained like a chimpanzee to do simple tricks. The Inauguration needed this kind of hysteria—a sea of tuxedoes and evening gowns doing the Wave. Think of it.

And accept this modest proposal for the next election. Make the Inauguration the Super Bowl half-time show. Prerecord the swearing-in, have the executive branch lip-synch their lines, mix it with a dance beat, and bring out the clean-cut All American breakdancers. A President is only inaugurated every four years; somebody should pay attention to it. And if the Super Bowl only happened every four years, or never, as far as that goes, well that'd be all right too.

Recovering, 2/1/85

Vampires on Bikes

There are still mysteries out there that can make even the pure of heart tremble. Pure of heart I'm not, the strength of ten has somehow escaped me (I'm not even sure I have the strength of one), but I think it's time to dust off the garlic and give the exorcist a call. Because vampires walk among us. Blood dopers. Olympic hopefuls.

Like that rock star who, it was rumored, tried to kick a drug habit by replacing his tainted blood with the blood of a Mexican boy, a small group of athletes tried to trade blood for gold. I can't speak to the legality of blood doping, but the whole notion strikes me as a bit, shall we say, creepy.

I guess even in this bland world, elements of the Gothic poke their gargoyle heads through the polyester fabric of our times. There are no pencil-sharp incisors here, no bats or murky castles. These vampires don't ride blood-red steeds on moonless nights, but slim bicycles in bright sunlight. They didn't take blood to stay alive (or, more properly, undead), they didn't bathe in the blood of virgins to improve their complexions. Neither decadent nor devilish, they merely took a small transfusion to gain a slight edge in a competition.

Isn't it strange that one of the oldest taboos in the civilized world is now par for the course? I'm the first to admit that when I look in the mirror the face of a sports fan does not stare back at me, but at least there's a reflection there. How about these jocks? Will they quake at the sight of a crucifix? Will the Nautilus equipment on which they spend their days be replaced by a coffin? Will they only bicycle at night?

America ran away with the gold, and it looks like we're trying to win the mad-doctor race as well. The Soviets have already developed hideous parodies of human beings, Frankenstein monsters half-human and half-steroid. How far can this go? Werewolf pole vaulters? Zombie decathlons? Will we only hold the Olympics on full-moon nights? There are some things man was not meant to know, and some things athletes weren't meant to mess with. If you need to sacrifice small animals in a pentangle just to shave a couple of microseconds off a timed event, maybe it's time to find a different line of work. Like sorcery. We've got enough athletes as it is. What the world needs now is a really good alchemist.

Waiting for Lugosi, 1/28/85

VIDEO

Coming Next Month

My idea of a good TV evening is watching all the movies I missed thirty years ago. Movies with titles like *I Married a Doctor, Empty Boots At Gun Hill, Last Bus Past the Johnson Farm, Zombie Nurse* and *Baltimore After Dark*. My idea of movie stars are people like Lyle Talbot, William Talbot, William Smith, Richard Carlson, Gloria Talbot, Richard Conte, Dane Clark, and Dana Andrews with (of course) Whit Bissell as the frightened dentist.

So maybe I'm not the guy to listen to, when I say I could have told you the TV networks would have to cancel most of their current season. Their problem is still (after all these years) that they don't have a handle on the twelve-year-old mindset. You'd think they'd learn from experience and get their scriptwriters fresh out of junior high, but well, I'm still a tweenager in my head, so here are a few ideas for the networks to get themselves ahead in the ratings wars.

You want series, networks? How about:

Celebrity Bill Collectors. In the pilot episode Robert Stack gets a rent check in Philadelphia and Joan Collins repossesses a Firebird in Great Neck.

UFO Hypnotist. Bill Bixby mesmerizes ordinary people to tell the UFO stories they probably would have told anyway.

If Simon McCorkindale's still available offer him *Alien Patrol*, or get Alan Alda for *General Bilko*. With the right star they could both take off. I've even got a treatment called *Kisses for My Poltergeist*, which would be perfect for a young Debbie Reynolds or an old Shelley Long.

The Bitter Monkees. After twenty years in show business, America's answer to the Fab Four tries again. In the pilot, the

Bitter Monkees have twelve mahogany doors slammed in their faces and fire their agent. It's hilarious, believe you me.

If you're a newshound and as big a Geraldo Rivera fan as I know I am, you might enjoy on Thursday, *News You Don't Want to Hear*. In this unique program Geraldo will unearth the hidden connection between organized crime and the cheese industry, he'll explore the pain of animal drug abuse, and examine the little-known phenomenon of transsexual out-of-body experiences. Plus celebrity interviews with Simon McCorkindale and Joan Collins.

No, I'm not forgetting the miniseries, even if I wish I could. How about *James Buchanan: The Man, the President*. It's got all the juicy stuff you never thought you wanted to know.

Or the twelve-hour epic *Pepsi: The Next Generation*, with *no* commercial interruptions.

I got game shows: *Trivia Amnesia*, in which contestants try their best to forget useless facts, and of course *Fast Food Divorce* with Judge Wapner and the gang.

Come on, media, make the checks payable to me, Ian Shoales. I'll have one eye glued to the mailbox, and the other glued either to *Celebrity Lifestyles of the Rich and Famous* or the *M*A*S*H* network. Twenty-four hours a day! All *M*A*S*H* all the time!

Reading TV Guide, *5/3/84*

Survivors

A survivor used to be a guy who didn't die when his plane crashed. A wavy-haired reporter in a three-piece suit would cram an imposing microphone into the survivor's face to ask a rude question guaranteed to trigger massive weeping from the survivor and massive channel switching from the rest of us, who'd rather watch *Three's Company* reruns than the anguish of some poor sap we've never even met. But the guy who doesn't die doesn't qualify as a survivor in the '80s. He's just more food for the hungry mouth of telecommunications. The survivor ain't in the hospital anymore—no, a survivor in the '80s is a guy with two hit series under his belt.

In the '80s the TV entertainer has a life so special and intense that a mere consumer can only be allowed brief hallucinatory glimpses of it. On the back pages of *People* Magazine some third-rate actor says, "I'm a survivor." You realize with shock that he's only talking about the hard time he's had adjusting to fame, as though fame were some sort of dread disease that only the lucky few survive. Survival means self-pity transformed by egotism into something awesomely creepy.

Here's the survivor: some bland actor, the hot new star of *Lotsa Cars on the Prairie*, replaces another bland actor, who was fired mid-season over a contract dispute. In the *TV Guide* interview there are discreet references to divorce, drugs, hassles with agents and fellow stars. It's not an easy road, he implies, but everything's better now, thanks to the special love of a special woman, invariably described as a "terrific" lady. *Terrific* is the survivor's favorite adjective, used to describe with equal enthusiasm people, food and emotional states. Just by studying the obviously staged photograph of this mediocre human being, surrounded by his special lady, his special poodles, his special shoes, all cavorting in the overheated pool— you can tell that this is one actor ready to join the ranks of the truly famous.

The truly famous are a terrific group of people. They get to write autobiographies or have them written, they get to put both feet in their mouths on talk shows, making ill-advised comments on controversial issues they know absolutely nothing about. The truly famous are the true survivors.

Shelley Winters is a survivor. Stewart Granger is not. Liza-with-a-z survived. Tiny Tim couldn't cut the mustard. Erik Estrada is a survivor. Bruce Jenner is not. Suzanne Somers ain't gonna make it, but Lynda Carter will. It remains to be seen whether the gals on *Charlie's Angels*—even the smart one—will survive. The ultimate survivor is Orson Welles, who is remembered less as a filmmaker today than as an amateur magician and drinker of dry table wines.

So how does a survivor die? Death is doing the guest spot on *Magnum P.I.* for scale. If you need the exposure, you're dead. Death is selling the second Porsche. Death is landing a cameo appearance as the third victim in a drive-in horror movie. Death is waiting by the drained pool for the calls that never come. Last year's officer on *Chips* parks cars for a living while millions of dolls bearing his likeness sell like hotcakes in shopping malls throughout the land. You're living out the zombie half-life of the once-famous, caressing your clippings, your videotapes as you sip your Margarita alone. You've run out of prime time. Your special lady has left you for this year's model. You're off the air, pal, and nobody remembers your name.

Express lane of Park and Shop, 5/15/82

Still the Beaver

When I was a kid I left it to the Beaver. I still do, watching *Leave It to Beaver* reruns on some UHF station at two on a rainy weekday afternoon. I watch cute little Beaver, squinting as though the TV lights hurt his eyes, screwing up his voice into that distinctive "Gee Wally" as he and big brother struggle unsuccessfully to keep their tiny problems from the just and merciful eyes of June and Ward. We should have let those sleeping dogs lie. We should have left June in the kitchen with her pearls and her apron, we should have left Ward with his unlit pipe and his mysterious job. When Beaver left for high school and Wally for college, we should have left them on that rocky road to the '60s. We should have lived with the bizarre rumors. Remember? Beaver died in Vietnam. Eddie Haskell was really Alice Cooper. Eddie Haskell was really John Holmes, the porno star.

But every bright success breeds a pale sequel. We've got a

new series now, a new program, a new product, *Still the Beaver*. Beaver in the '80s, all grown up, Jerry Mathers as thirty-five-year-old Beaver, divorced, with a child of his own. Farewell sweetness and light, farewell suburbia, goodbye Miss Landers, Whitey, Lumpy, farewell. Beaver's an adult, he's made his own deal, he's landed his own series. We'll know what Beaver does for a living (we never knew what Ward did), and the grown-up Beaver won't wear a tie to dinner, or those cardigan sweaters with patches on the elbows. We'll know more about Beaver than we want to know. Goodbye pearls in the garden, goodbye pearls of middle-class wisdom. We're in the '80s now. Beaver's as old as I am, and he's got the same problems. I don't want to know about it. The whole concept seems to have been dreamed up by Eddie Haskell, the Satan of *Leave It to Beaver* land, the snake in Miss Landers' apple.

Eddie Haskell's grown up too; he's become a television producer. He's producing *Still the Beaver*. Divorce, aging and sorrow have marched into Mayfield. The gates are closing on Cleaverville, Archieville, Mayberry, the emerald kingdom of Ozzie and Harriett, where the lawns went on forever, and winter never touched. The sunlight still comes through the venetian blinds to make stripes on the wall-to-wall carpeting, but now we see the motes of dust, we see the signs of wear. I don't want to see it. I don't want to be updated on Beaver in the '80s. I think the curtain has fallen on those gauzy '50s lives. The story's over. I don't want to know the rest. Leave Beaver alone.

In Joe's, watching Disney channel, 2/1/85

Breakdancing

A cigarette commercial years ago showed a happy defiant smoker with a black eye and the caption, "Us Tareyton smokers would rather fight than switch." A strange message—"If you smoke these cigarettes someone will punch you in the face," but I guess it sold a lot of tobacco, because when they brought out their low-tar cigarettes, the ad showed a happy smoker, white-out painted under the eye, and the caption, "Us Tareyton smokers would rather light than fight," which made absolutely no sense at all, except as a comment on the first ad, and if you never saw the first ad, you'd have no idea what was being said. That's okay; it's as good a way as any to discourage smoking, but it just goes to show—making sense is overrated and will never sell a product.

Our advertising industry is always on the lookout for that elusive quality called the lowest common denominator, and they're not choosey where they find it. If it's not nailed down, anything unique will get turned into a selling point, and breakdancing is no exception. Breakdancing is genuine folk art and, as such, anonymous. Nobody took out a patent on breakdancing. The black kids on the street who invented the moonwalk were involved in a collaboration that will never be recognized with royalties or awards. Instead, it moved *up* in the culture. And the end result is clean-cut white kids break-dancing for clothing chains.

Any special regional or racial character trait which creates or exhibits genuine personality gets melted down into a comfort-able image designed for the sole purpose of selling something. Thus, we see a Vermont accent used in maple-syrup commercials, we see farm folks and Gramps pushing orange juice or cereal. If we need a testimonial from "real people," we go to Indiana or Ohio, where everybody talks like an astronaut, to lend credence to claims for headache remedies or bleach.

If there is such a thing as "trickle-down" economics, this is my "trickle-up" theory of pop culture. It's not really thievery, since accents and natural exuberance are not copyrightable. Until human grace gets a lawyer, kids on the street and the normal joe will continue to be victims of a nameless exploitation. Any real relish for life will be transformed into *gusto*. Any manifestation of joy will turn up next month as a beer commercial.

Watching commercials, 1/25/85

Winds of War

The weather's too drizzly for a guy like me, who needs a four-figure advance to get out of bed, much less go outside. Until the rain stops I've been spending my days in bed, watching my little television. Imagine my surprise last night when a voice like Winston Churchill's spoke to me from my television. It asked, "Who turned World War II into a great home video game?"

I about dropped my malt liquor. "Who turned World War II into a great home video game?" Let's tackle this question, folks. Number one, I don't like it when my TV talks to me; I can't talk back. Number two, I don't think I want to know who turned World War II into a home video game, much less a *great* one. Number three, I don't like the idea that someone had the *idea* to turn World War II into a great home video game. Number four, I don't like the idea that someone used a bad imitation of Winston Churchill's voice to sell us the idea that World War II has been turned into a great home video game. Number five, the whole idea is outlandish, useless, bizarre and appalling. The whole idea is an idea from hell. If I hadn't been watching Matt Houston at the time, I would have thrown my television out the window—if I had a window.

I know that Nazis are America's new hobby, the perfect subject for any miniseries, and loud noises and bright colors are America's idea of entertainment, but when *The Winds of War* is watched by more people than fought the war, I start to wonder. And *The Winds of War* wasn't even about World War II, it was about a remarkably unpleasant American family, trapped by farfetched plot twists in events beyond their control. Poor Robert Mitchum had to dash all over the world so he could meet Churchill, Roosevelt and Hitler; and still try to squeeze in time to understand his psychotic son. Mitchum was catatonic, but no wonder the guy looked sleepy. A lot of perfectly good media sarcasm has already been wasted on Ali

McGraw, so I'll leave her out of this, and simply ask: what happened to low-budget war movies?

There are oodles of no-talent actors out there looking for a break. Let's go back to those black-and-white movies about six unshaven guys slogging through a muddy back lot. Frank Lovejoy and Audie Murphy chain-smoking unfiltered cigarettes in a dank foxhole. Sarge and Gunner, Tex, The Kid, the guy from Brooklyn, a handful of dirty buddies, their Tommy guns blazing, blasting their way through the Kraut lines, into Berlin *singlehanded*, and no Ali McGraw in sight. Or Winston Churchill either. To hell with historical accuracy and to hell with great home video games. If I want historical accuracy I'll go to the library. If I want a video game I'll go to the mall. Just as soon as this rain lets up.

One week in March '83

News Anchors

Nightline. Ted Koppel's mildly amused face floats before us as he states the theme of the show (unemployment, terrorism—the subject varies night to night, but the format stays the same). We move to the news clips, the updates, then back to Ted and the interviews with the experts and pundits of the world, and Ted isn't even in the same room with them. The video images of the people being talked to hang in the rear like talking portraits, disembodied heads. It's surreal, but Ted Koppel moves the talk along. Ted Koppel is a tiny god. He has the power. Ted Koppel is the news anchor.

The news anchor anchors down the images we see. The anchor is the soothing presence we can always return to, like Mommy after a nightmare, the friendly cop after a mugging. The anchor keeps us from drowning in the airwaves, keeps us from crashing on the rocks of bad news. As the sails fill with the winds of war, as we drift from war-torn port to port in the distressed Global Village, we know that the anchor is at the helm, as amused as Ted Koppel, bemused as David Brinkley, stern as Dan Rather, avuncular as Walter Cronkite. The anchor is our eyes, our roots, our anchor in the deep, still waters of the news.

And we need a human face in the face of all that suffering. Sure the advertisements offer us portholes on a more attractive artificial world, but we always return to Beirut, Salvador, Nicaragua, and we must have that familiar face to steer us, an undamaged face, someone the news can't touch. Even MTV has a TV DJ we return to between the smash hits, so we won't think the images are random. Because television *is* random. Video is a hungry mouth devouring information and images, it doesn't matter what—Falklands crisis or *Loveboat* episode, cop or killer, *Fantasy Island* or Fidel's island, the reporters are sailors in their drip-dry suits, the actors are sailors in their blow-dried hair. Quincy, Johnny, Alice, Ted are faces bobbing in the waves. Television is just a window on a piece of furniture, a window on a cruel world, where people are killed for no apparent reason, where unseen audiences laugh at unfunny jokes. The world may sleep, but television never sleeps. I watch it till my eyes grow heavy. I watch it till I drown, anchored on the couch. Television is a daily dark vicarious voyage on the waves both old and new. It never stops, it just fades away. I turn it off at midnight, the screen grows dark, a pale pinpoint of light diminishes slowly in the center of the tube, an artificial sun going down in a dark and nameless sea.

On the couch, 11/12/83

TV Violence

I have to admit I pretty much stopped watching network television when *Rockford Files* went off the air. But from what I've read, psychologists and worried Moms have a point: network TV is too violent. Network TV promotes a world view at odds with reality. Sure. Tell me something new.

It's true, our founding fathers didn't exactly have television in mind when they wrote the Bill of Rights. They didn't have it back then, you know; if they had, they probably would have done the Bill of Rights as a video, or more probably surrendered to the British then and there. The British have conquered us now anyway, at least on MTV. Duran Duran has succeeded where King George failed.

On the other hand, I hate to have to point this out, but nobody forced us to buy TV sets. One of the sacred freedoms in this country is the God-given right *not* to buy something. I know, you're saying, "We have them now, we're stuck with them." And you're probably also right when you imply that every violent crime in this country is the fault either of the television industry or of education. Guns don't kill people, television kills people.

And since we do possess the God-given right to possess handguns (I'm sure it's in the Bible somewhere), and the subsequent God-given right to gun each other down in stupid domestic squabbles, and since registration of handguns is the first step toward confiscation, which leads, of course, to Naziism, Communism, and the end of the known universe—I would say the time has come to do something about television. What other choice do we have?

I recommend, first of all, a battery of psychiatric evaluation tests for each and every would-be TV purchaser. Try this sample question:

When you see a rerun of *Charlie's Angels*, do you

    a. Drool.
    b. Switch the channel.
    c. Harbor vague thoughts about remodeling the living room.
    d. Have a sudden desire to get off the couch and kill all living creatures with a chainsaw.

I realize a crafty psycho might answer "a" to throw you off the scent, so the test would have to be organized by experts.

Remember if every psychotic in this country has Remote Capability, only moral chaos can follow.

If we can't get the psychology together, at least get an IQ test. An IQ of over 100 gets you a black-and-white, over 120 you get color, over 130 if you want cable or VCR. This is absolutely necessary. Otherwise we'll have to outlaw television. When TV is outlawed, only outlaws will have TV.

And a nation that can't tell the difference between their television screens and their lives deserves everything that happens to them.

Shopping for a VCR, 10/1/84

Taboo!

Now this: Taboos! Forbidden desires! Film at eleven. Next: *Tawny: Portrait of a Teenage Runaway Incestuous Hooker.* Tonight, Cagney and Lacey teach a male stripper would-be rapist spokesmodel how to care. Tonight on *Hill Street Blues*, alcoholic child molesters lurk beyond the threshold of a typical American family. Tonight! EyeCenter Eleven focuses on battered women trapped in a world they never made. Taboos! More information. All the time.

See Loni Anderson pretend to be terrified. Lynda Carter becomes frightened of her own hair. Tonight at ten. Then: Are artists insane? New facts reveal that one out of every five Americans is mentally ill and *doing nothing about it.*

The agony of love or the bliss of rage? Join us on *20/20* for a revealing look at what psychologists say could be a new problem—police informants with disguised voices. Then, Mr. T. takes a look at more zany antics, as celebrities play pranks on normal people. It's *Plumbers of the Stars!* Then:

What is the dark secret shared by these impossibly beautiful women? Information and entertainment collide as *Sixty Minutes* takes a look at the copywriting approach to real problems, right here on the Hype and Silliness Network. Then: a major corporation talks to you as if it were a person and you could talk back, as Mobil looks at images in politics in *The Media in Politics*.

Vanessa Williams and Vanessa Redgrave in *Portrait of Two Vanessas*. Then it's time for *Another Girlfriend of Howard Hughes*, then *Battle of the Porno Stars!* We'll meet a man who's had a camera installed in his head on *Real Cute Old People*.

Is there lunch after marriage? Is there happiness after lunch? Find out on *Forbidden Taboos!*

She was a preteen undercover cop. He was a lingerie salesman with a cocaine problem. Together they're dynamite, as teenage hookers go after T.J. Hooker on *Stupid Jokes and Blunders*, then a troubled Vietnam vet drifts from network to network in the touching first-time-on-television première of *Looking for a Writer*.

We bid a fond farewell to the printed word on *Nails in the IQ Coffin* tonight! Next: Hollywood takes a look at Hollywood taking a look at America as *Entertainment Tonight* examines *Eye On Hollywood* who take you behind the scenes of network news, as they cover the story of how television is made.

Truth and lies and issues and images on *Is America Insane?* Writers and actors search for meaning on *The Ratings War*, a new endless miniseries tonight on all three networks.

Just because you found a problem doesn't mean you get a reward. Just because you can tell a good lie doesn't mean you're an artist. Secrets! Taboos! Tonight! Now this! Then! Next!

Flipping the dial, 12/10/84

CINEMA

Teenagers

You don't normally think of Alexander the Great as a teenager, but the fact is he conquered the world at an age when most of us were still trying to find a summer job. Think of the epic lads and lasses through history: Heloïse and Abelard, Romeo and Juliet, Mozart, Rimbaud, Shelley, Keats, Laura Ingalls Wilder. They were young, tragic, romantic—they were pioneers. Two hundred years ago it was tuberculosis that carried away the young. Tuberculosis, a disease much admired by the Romantics, was analogous to the car accident of the 1950s. It was the tragic flaw of flaming youth, proof that you were larger than life. You lived fast, died young and left a beautiful corpse.

Teenagers once had the good sense to die young, like Sal Mineo in *Rebel Without a Cause*. He was too sensitive for the world. If they didn't die young, at least they saved the world from space aliens, like Steve McQueen in *The Blob;* or they actually *became* monsters (young Michael Landon in *I Was a Teenage Werewolf*) which is about as Misunderstood as Youth can get. In the '70s modern teens found even more creative ways to die, at the hands of murdering psychopaths in movies like *Hallowe'en* and *Friday the 13th*. It was all part of an ancient Western tradition.

But now it's come to an end. In movies like *Porky's* and *Animal House*, the Dustin Hoffman figure of the '60s is not merely confused he's emotionally retarded. In movie after movie, young teenage boys are just seeking brief glimpses of a young woman's undraped female bosom, the sight of which sends the teenage boy into a leering lust so intense that he actually faints, or at least falls down.

Even stranger, the teenage girls take their shirts off at every given opportunity. Why? Where's the thrill? They take off their shirts—bam! The boyfriend faints dead away. Whose idea of a sexual relationship is this? It's not promiscuity and it's not repression either. It's something different—a side effect of the sexual revolution.

I blame the Republicans, who were so afraid a teacher or parent might let a kid in on the secrets of procreation, that a woman's body has once again attained the kind of mythical dimensions that it had in Greek myths, wherein a mortal glimpsing the goddess bathing in the sacred grove would be struck blind. It's the woman's body as Medusa's head.

All right, there's no war right now for the young man of today, but there is something wrong when the only rite of passage available to the young American male is through the turnstiles of these incredibly stupid movies. It's just a milk gland, kids, come on, get it together.

In line at the Cineplex, 9/19/83

That Dog's Gonna Die

Let's talk movies, let's talk cinematic experience. Jimmy Stewart's pal, usually Walter Brennan, gets wasted by Dan Duryea, forcing Jimmy to dust off the Colts and go to town. In *The Wild Bunch* General Mapache killed Angel, and the Wild Bunch killed everything in sight. Give the hero a friend, a dog, a girlfriend, a little handicapped boy with learning disabilities; then kill the dog, and the hero's ready for battle. Good suffers, then Good is redeemed in combat. This is what I call the That-Dog's-Gonna-Die school of screenwriting.

James Bond's first girlfriend (Shirley Eaton in *Goldfinger*) is always killed by the villain. Innocent children drop like flies in Billy Jack movies. Even in *Last Picture Show*, as soon as the retarded boy began to sweep the streets I knew he was a goner. Screenwriters love to kill off harmless creatures for the sake of the plot line. Finding the scapegoat is half the fun. *The Road Warrior:* The bad guys killed the warrior's dog, and warrior killed the bad guys. *Blue Thunder:* Bad guys killed Roy Scheider's pal, Roy killed the bad guys.

I thought I had *Return of the Jedi* figured out. Skywalker was going to get wasted in a sacrifice play, so Han would get the girl and the rebels would get the galaxy. Bye-bye Luke. That dog's gonna die. But *Return of the Jedi* wasn't even true to its own clichés. The only thing that died were robots and muppets, and you can fix robots, they don't even count.

If you haven't seen *Return of the Jedi* I'm sorry if I ruined an incredibly dull experience for you, but it ruined my whole That-Dog's-Gonna-Die theory of screenwriting. Not only that, but Darth Vader unmasked looked exactly like Uncle Fester on *The Addams Family.* I don't know what that means, but if that's all the dark side of the force can come up with, we sure live in a bland universe. You might as well let the dog live.

In line for Tootsie, *1/5/85*

The Little Person

Except for *Road Warrior*, which I've seen twelve times, I usually don't go to Australian movies. If I see the preview for an Australian movie, I feel like I've already seen the movie. But I went to see *The Year of Living Dangerously*, because (like *Under Fire*, a great movie) it showed journalists in a state of confusion. I love to see confused journalists anywhere, but that's not what I want to talk about.

I want to talk about Linda Hunt's Oscar. She did a great job, and deserves any award that comes her way, but her role in *Living Dangerously* was the same role given to so-called "dwarves and midgets" since the beginning of literature. This role is, near as I can put it, the tortured conscience of man. It was the same role Michael Dunne played in *Ship of Fools*, only he was the life force of pre-WWII Europe, or Oscar in *The Tin Drum* representing the stunted heart of WWII Germany.

Writers from Edgar Allen Poe to Carson McCullers have used little people as stand-ins for the "little guy." Or they're used for comic effect, or to make Ricardo Montalban look taller. Or they're a symbol of decadence on rock videos, cute and magical in *Wizard of Oz*, they're a stand-in for aliens in *E.T.* In *Poltergeist* and *Don't Look Now*, they were psychic and psychotic respectively.

Little people are used as a symbol for some kind of oogie-boogie connection to the collective unconscious. Well, I guess being a symbol isn't a bad job as far as it goes (though personally I thought allegories went out of literary style in the late Middle Ages, excepting certain *Twilight Zone* episodes), but if I were a little person and an actor, I'd want more out of my career than symbolizing the sick soul of modern man on one hand, or making a hunk of *Star Wars* tin move on the other hand. Little people lead lives like the taller rest of us, they have kids, they work downtown—how about it, Hollywood? Why not cast little people as *people?* It's not too much to ask. If you want a symbol of decadence and alienation, why not use Dustin Hoffman? He'd probably like the challenge and be grateful for the change of pace.

Not Down Under, 4/15/83

Bond. James Bond

President Kennedy, my hero when I was twelve years old, turned me on to James Bond. When I read in *Time* that Kennedy read him I had to read him too. When a new Bond arrived at the library I would beg Miss Larson to let me check it out. She said it was adult reading and smiled her gold-and-silver smile, her reading glasses bouncing on the shelf of her bosom like a strange necklace. Let me clue you, I've read 'em all, pals and gals: 007 is not adult reading.

I remember the paperback of *Dr. No*. The Signet edition had a flat-black cover with a tiny picture in the center: Bond protecting a cowering woman from Dr. No's flame-throwing death machine. On the back cover was a picture of the aging imperialist himself, Ian Fleming, the last of the "Old Boy" Britishers (looking like he had stepped from the pages of a Le Carré novel), smoking a cigarette in a holder, and nonchalantly holding a large pistol. There you have it, kids, the British smoothie with a license to kill was written *by* a stunted adolescent *for* stunted adolescents. A martini shaken not stirred, a fast Bentley, a Walther P-38—this insane catalogue of detail appeals to twelve-year-old boys and readers of men's magazines, not adults.

President Kennedy is gone, Fleming is gone, but Bond lives on, getting bigger with every movie, and the *outré* villains, the women with one name like Solitaire or Domino—they get bigger too. Through cold war, assassinations, upheaval, Vietnam, the Falklands, Bond has strolled through his overblown adventures with arched eyebrows: the ultimate fantasy figure of a dying empire.

Women and gadgets are both drawn to him—in *Goldfinger* (the novel) even a lesbian is drawn back by Bond into the heterosexual fold. Q gives him gadgets; he saves the world with them and throws them away, *smashes* them, drives them over cliffs. When the world is safe the women disappear too. Bond is the ultimate consumer, saving the world from major destruction so he can enjoy the pleasure of his minor destructions. That world will never end. No buttons will be pushed as long as Bond is around. Arrogant and modest at the same time, he saves the world with a shrug.

As long as boys need heroes, we'll have James Bond. As an aging American boy I look back at Bond with mixed feelings. Or maybe my feelings aren't mixed. After twenty-five years of James Bond, maybe my feelings are the same as his martinis—shaken, not stirred.

On reading Dr. No *for the tenth time, 7/7/83*

John Travolta's Body

I can't escape John Travolta's body. I'm waiting in the market express lane, with a six of malt liquor—and there's that shaved and oiled shape on the cover of hip journals, bourgeois scandal sheets, on the cover of everything but *The New York Review Of Books*. All right, John Travolta looks good with no shirt on. But he's got a gravity guider, a body-building system, indoor heated pool, sauna, Jacuzzi, hot tub, clothes, a ruddy Swedish masseuse named Olga; he can *afford* to eat well, dress well, he's got the leisure time to stay in shape. In the world Travolta lives in, he can do anything, or have someone do it for him. That body on display is a body of knowledge on display. He's a living collaboration, a work of art, a sculpture, a movie star, a product selling itself. The knowledge implicit in creating that naked display could fill an encyclopedia. Like moths to the flame, knowledge is drawn to John Travolta's body. And that's just one image. And that's just the surface of what we know.

We can build H-bombs or read Sylvia Plath. We know the difference between a byte and a bit. We've got the perfect martini and people on the moon. We've got experts on contract bridge, nutrition, flashbulbs and photostats, clothespins and wheels, statistics, logistics, minicams and sitcoms—we know too much for our own good and enough is enough. The last person to know *everything* was Leonardo da Vinci. Let's stop. Let's declare a moratorium on knowledge and experience. Let's stop accumulating and start assimilating.

I don't want to compare my pale skinny body to John Travolta's as I sit shirtless before the TV waiting for the all-night movie to start. I don't want to remember the secret ingredients of fourteen brands of soap. Let's go totally generic. Generic is soothing to the eye and saves money. White boxes with the name of the product in plain type—soap, cigarettes, movie star. Let's stop getting sold a bill of goods. Let's learn

155

what the technocrats and bureaucrats know, and let them learn from us—how to get up, how to get *down*. Let's take a vacation from learning until all of us know what some of us know. Ronald Reagan reading *High Times*, John Travolta reading *Scientific American*. Let's work for a world of fit, well-read Renaissance men and women. Put clothes back on the naked body of knowledge, clothes on the emperor. Let's make John Travolta put his shirt back on. Experts have been running numbers on us long enough. Let's get their number, and then move on.

In the express lane, 8/15/83

Blockbusters

I know that nostalgia is to memory what diet soda is to fine Chablis, so I hope I'm popping a cork and not a pop top when I say there hasn't been a decent summer movie since *Creature from the Black Lagoon*. That movie had everything: Love. Adventure. Evolution. Movie monsters don't fall in love with earthling women anymore. The monsters in movies today are all too human and only enjoy slicing up naked teenagers with common garden tools. Most of the movies I remember enjoying as a kid were in black and white and seemed to star either Glenn Ford or Audie Murphy.

There was no such thing as a remake, prequel, or sequel. Every Audie Murphy movie was the same, but who cared? Watching a familiar face clench his jaw through his familiar low-budget paces was part of the charm. Now, when I sit in the quadruplex cinderblock mall hole, eating cold popcorn with butter *flavoring*, sipping tepid sodas with a bunch of strangers, where the sound track from the movie next door drowns out the movie I'm watching, watching millions of Hollywood bucks go by in a flash, it doesn't seem like a movie anymore, so much as the visual aftermath of a series of bad corporate decisions.

Face it. A movie hero is just a guy who looks good on a

horse, only now the horse has been replaced by a space ship, and our hero takes home a cool mil per flick. Steve Reeves may have been replaced by Arnold Schwarzenegger, and Jeff Chandler by Harrison Ford, but the crop of summer movies is the same silly crop I harvested as a kid, only with ten times the budget and no butter for the popcorn. Even a simple fistfight today requires special makeup, choreographers, stunt men, exploding blood bags, and more munitions experts than the Green Berets. In the '50s all you needed for a fistfight was a thin line of chocolate syrup which would trickle from the side of the mouth of the hero as he stood triumphant over the unconscious body of Dan Duryea.

Take a chance on me, Mr. Spielberg. I've got my finger on the pulse of America, and believe me, the patient is not well. I just happen to have written the remake of *Creature from the Black Lagoon*. The screenplay's burning a hole in my drawer. What have you got to lose? All you need is a $10,000 budget, a gallon or two of chocolate syrup and of course, a frog suit, extra large.

On seeing Temple of Doom *for the sixth time, 5/22/84*

The Big Chill

I have a lawyer girlfriend who leaps into masochistic moods with both feet. When in Suffer mood she usually drags me to an Ingmar Bergman movie, where I endure endless healthy Swedish faces, filling the screen with ruddy self-pity; or she takes me to coffeehouses where morose feminists read monotonous odes to joy. These little doses of bland avant-garde seem to make her feel better for some reason.

In one of those moods last week she dragged me to see *The Big Chill*. The title suggests Raymond Chandler, but the dialogue isn't hard-bitten, just hard to swallow—the kind of writing we're told is good, but isn't, the kind of self-conscious dialogue that tells us more than we want to know.

And *The Big Chill* has no Bogart, just good-looking Hollywood people pretending to be people just like us, only more successful: sipping fine white wines, smoking incredibly well-rolled sticks of the finest marijuana, and reeling off semiwitty phrases about where their lives have gone since the '60s. *The Big Chill* just sits on the screen because these people aren't going anywhere. They've arrived. They're in the full blossom of self-pity. They're in their middle thirties and acting like their lives are over. *The Big Chill* is a movie about and made by all the people I hated in high school. They were hipper and smarter than I was then, and they make more money than I do now. Not only that, they feel guiltier than I do.

An article in *Esquire* a few issues back said: "Years after the war, the relief many of the Vietnam generation felt at having evaded the military has been supplanted by shame. These nonveterans must suddenly heal wounds they never knew they had."

Not only is this insulting to veterans who are healing wounds they know damn well they had, it's insulting to people like me who squeezed out of the draft and are damn proud of it.

What, are we dead already? Did our lives end in 1970? Is everything we've done since then just one long betrayal of half-thought-out youthful ideals? Are we just slim attractive cattle sitting around our *Architectural Digest* homes chewing the cud of the poisoned past? I say no, ladies and gentlemen, and leave you with a warning:

Pals and gals, our generation is fast on its way to becoming the most insubstantial group of human beings who ever trod the face of the planet. Don't we have anything better to do than sit around and feel sorry for ourselves over things that did or didn't happen fifteen, twenty years ago? What do you say, kids. Time to grow up?

On the couch, 9/15/83

Red Dawn

When I was a kid I saw a movie called *The Time Machine* about a guy who travels to the future, saves the world from monsters and falls in love with a gal named Weena. About two minutes before the movie started I happened to punch the local bully right in front of the popcorn stand. Expectation of his retaliation kind of put an edge to full cinematic enjoyment. The movie made me wish I had a time machine, not to travel to the future, but to go back in time and take back the punch.

Time and the movie, however, marched on. The hero went back, or forward, I suppose, to his Weena, I snuck out the rear exit, where the guy I punched and two of his pals threw me down and beat the cheese out of me. I may have been outnumbered, but not outclassed. Even as their fists came down, I called them Communists at the top of my lungs. This caused them to hit me harder, of course, but they were weeping as they punched, and screaming at me to take it back, which just goes to show you the relative power of the word.

These sordid memories leaped into my head recently with the release of the first PG-13 movie, called *Red Dawn*. It's a fantasy about high-school kids fighting a Commie invasion in America's backyard, and it seems like it was written by my childhood bully. I always thought he'd grow up to be one of those overweight guys with slight asthma who subscribe to *Soldier of Fortune*, a guy who stays up all night hoping for a burglar so he can blow him away, a guy who bought a home just so he'd have something to defend. A handgun owner. A survivalist. When guys like that aren't busy shooting each other in household accidents, they're proposing scenarios to the local talk shows just like *Red Dawn*.

Kids love these apocalyptic visions, where the world as we know it has ended, the enemy is up close, it's you or them, get 'em in the gunsights, punch 'em in the eye. I went for it myself as a kid. It was me on the prairie with Dad's .22

scouting the horizon for Soviet tanks. My father's refusal to build a backyard fallout shelter struck me as proof positive of America's decadence in the face of an overwhelming faceless aggressor. But I was a kid. Why a grown man would believe this stuff is beyond me, and *Red Dawn* doesn't have a trace of irony.

So maybe *Red Dawn* is part of a pop-culture time machine. If we can declare this the Year of the Bible, or National Secretary's Week, why don't we make the unofficial official, and start over? Let's bring back the fifties.

We've already got self-conscious nostalgia all over the place—rockabilly revivals, '50s styles and fashions, flag-waving, even punks—the '80s equivalent of the juvenile delinquent. We can lose the silly things of the '80s—men's underwear for women, Cabbage Patch dolls, the invasion of Grenada—and go back to the real issues: cold war, fear and firecrackers, prayer in school, polio, and the hula hoop. Bring the nation back to the '50s and bring your guns along. I'd like to go with you, but I'd better stay here and guard your back. Let me know when you're ready. I'll be right here. In the fallout shelter. With Weena.

In the shelter, 8/14/84

Bye-bye L.A.

Where I come from, the word *creative* is used to describe six-year-olds who like to smear finger paint on the wall. In L.A., *creative* can describe just about anything: a lawyer's deal, a producer's package, a concept, a late brunch and tanning session. They even have "creative consultants" in L.A. What that *means* is anybody's guess. It's hard to figure out what anybody does in L.A., besides leave messages and drive.

I came to L.A. to stimulate mild interest in my screenplay. It's the thinly veiled and highly exaggerated story of my life, written in a heady style that combines the hard bite of Raymond Chandler and the tiny bark of Eve Babitz. I wanted Peckinpah to direct, of course, but now I'll take Altman. I'll even sell an option, which (if you don't know) is like paying a farmer not to grow crops. If a producer "options" a screenplay, it means he doesn't want it really, but he doesn't want anybody else to have it, and the screenplay will gather interest and dust on somebody's floppy disc. Fine with me, if I get paid.

But after two days on pay telephones, bright promises seem as false as a weatherman's prediction of acceptable air quality. The ear hurts, the eyes sting. The L.A. sky is a gray bowl tinged with pink. Smog blankets the city, a comfort in a way—smog keeps L.A. contained, shut off from the weather of the rest of the world. Because L.A. scares you and calms you down at the same time. It's the last home for those who harbor last hopes. America stops in L.A. After L.A. there's nothing but sharks, deep water, and Hawaiian condos. For desperate Okies and divorcees, would-be writers and movie stars, street people, and musicians, L.A. is the end of the line.

Yesterday I took my first meeting. I was greeted at the glass doors by an unnaturally tan young man, who ushered me into a simulated-walnut conference room. All the executives were sitting around a table roughly the size of Delaware. They all wore stereo headsets and were eating fruit. I was handed my headset and we listened to Bruce Springsteen tapes.

One of the execs shouted over the music to ask if I thought Springsteen was right to do the scores. Another one asked how well I knew Bruce Springsteen. When a third executive asked if I'd be interested in doing a treatment for *The Bruce Springsteen Story,* I got fed up. I ripped off my headset and said, "I'm not interested in Bruce Springsteen's life. It's hard enough to stay interested in *my* life. Here's the bottom line"—executives love it when you say "bottom line" in meetings—"I want Ricky Schroeder to play Ian as a boy, Richard Gere plays Ian as a man, and I get to date Kathleen Turner. And we gotta have music in this thing, make it David

Byrne or Philip Glass, so we can capture that art-house crowd and get a mixed review in *The Village Voice*. I wanna shoot it in black and white and I wanna dedicate the film to the memory of the late great Warren Oates."

There was a moment of silence. A Creative Consultant hefted my screenplay and asked, "What makes this a movie?" I snorted and said, "Fifty million bucks and a camera." Well, that was that. They had had enough of me. I'm the first person in L.A. history to get physically evicted from a meeting. The nut-brown secretary sneered at my pallor all the way down to the onyx lobby.

L.A.: where there's never weather, and walking is a crime. L.A.: where the streetlights and palm trees go on forever, where darkness never comes, like a deal that never goes down, a meeting that's never taken. The city of angels: where every cockroach has a screenplay and even the winos wear roller skates. It's that kind of town. Creative. Bye-bye, L.A.

Waiting for a plane, 11/15/83

Hearts and Bumpers

I'm not one of those tongue-clucking grammarians who leap on split infinitives or misplaced modifiers like a mongoose on a cobra. I'm not even much of a reader—I skim magazines, stopping now and then to sneer at some scorn-worthy nugget. I'll force a few pages of *Wired* into my brain before I get fed up and throw the book across the room. I've leafed through the *New York Review of Books* from time to time to see what new twelve-volume biography of Vita Sackville-West has been unleashed on an eager reading public.

I used to think that bleeding-heart mourners of literacy were beneath my contempt, and believe me, my contempt will stoop to anything. Those who complain that nobody reads anymore usually mean nobody reads *me, boo hoo*. And what's there to read anyway? One more self-conscious novel about a novelist trying to write a novel? One more *New Yorker* short story packed with brand names about brooding divorcees in New England? A novelization? Any jerk who reads a paperback version of a movie deserves professional help, not our pity.

I can handle reading T-shirts, the Kiss-Me-I'm-Polish T-shirt, the My-folks-went-to-Disneyland-and-all-they-bought-me-was-this-lousy-T-shirt T-shirt, the obscene-message-to-the-Ayatollah-that-the-Ayatollah-will-never-see-but-the-jerk's-wearing-the-T-shirt-anyway T-shirt. I can handle bumper stickers: I brake for animals, honk if you love Jesus, honk if you *are* Jesus, if you don't like the way I drive stay off the sidewalk—I can handle all this. If you want to advertise your half-baked beliefs on your body, or plaster unfunny used jokes on a moving vehicle, that's your business, and after all, bumper stickers and T-shirts are *the* prose form of the '80s, but I gotta draw the line, folks.

This heart business has me in a cold sweat. You know what I'm talking about: I heart NY. I heart S.F. I heart L.A. I heart my dog head.

It's got me buffaloed. What is being said? You love New York? So what? Who cares? You love your dog? Are you afraid people would think you didn't love your dog if you didn't have the bumper sticker? Why do you want people driving behind you to know you have a dog? Why is this important to you? Are you sure you love your dog? Do you in actual fact *hate* your dog? Did you hate your dog before you got the heart-your-dog-head bumper sticker, but now you love the mangy fleabag? Do you even have a damn dog? Maybe it's just wishful thinking. If you do have a dog and you do love it, why don't you just stick your head out the car window and yell, "I love my dog!" At least there'd be some passion, not this dimwitted graphic equivalent of baby talk, this so-cute-it's-creepy shorthand designed for not very bright three-year-olds, or Neanderthals. Write it out, shout it out, but throw those damn hearts away. Burn 'em. Get your heart off your bumper and back on your sleeve.

In a jam, 8/14/84

Modern Writers

When I read a book I want a couple of things. First, that the book tell the truth about the world or, failing that, give me a beautiful lie. Second, that the book fit on my bookshelf. I'm not getting these things from modern writers. Books these days are either so large they don't fit on my bookshelf, books made only for the coffee table, or they're so slim you might mistake them for a volume of poetry, and I don't like poetry, unless it's John Berryman. All other poets are wimps.

Joan Didion's new book *Salvador* is a slim volume you

might think is poetry until you read it. Ms. Didion has long been in the habit of finding little ironies for us, and parading them by us as if they meant something. *Salvador* is no disappointment to the admirers of Ms. Didion's thought processes, but she's become another victim of the *Apocalypse Now* syndrome, another modern writer on a search for horror, for situations we can't do anything about, to give us books that tell us things we already know.

What does Joan Didion finally tell us about El Salvador? She says it's confusing and scary down there. I don't have Ms. Didion's prose style or migraines or paranoia, but *I* could have told you it's confusing and scary in El Salvador, and I've never been there.

What's wrong with today's writers? The whole thing started with Hunter Thompson's *Fear And Loathing In Las Vegas*, in which Thompson took every hallucinogen known to man, then dashed around Vegas all stoned and goggle-eyed at the *fin-de-siècle* neon decadence. Of course, it made him paranoid. What did he expect? If you go someplace scary, you're going to get scared.

From Norman Mailer to Tom Wolfe, *Rolling Stone* to *Esquire* it's "Look at me, I'm expressing myself," "Look at me, I'm in the same room as a rock star," "Look at me, I'm hip and I'm paranoid." The New Journalism's getting old, folks. If I'm going to have these weird-shaped books in my house, let it be Jane Fonda's *Workout Book*. The prose is terrible, but at least there's lots of pictures to throw darts at. Throw darts at the New Journalists, the only thing you'll puncture is Norman Mailer's ego, whose career has just been capped by *Ancient Evenings*, which is perhaps the silliest novel ever published.

At the library, 5/12/83

CIA Murder Manual

The so-called CIA assassination manual probably won't make the best-seller lists, but it wouldn't surprise me if it did. We've already got how-to books about sex, eating, and making it in the business world, why not a how-to book on murder? And the CIA is the ideal author. Lying and murder (or to put it bureaucratically, disinformation and termination) in the national interest are part of the CIA tradition: The Bay of Pigs, Chile, Guatemala, even a bizarre plot to smoke Fidel with a poison cigar—all are part of the proud accomplishments (or in CIA lingo, disaccomplishments) of the CIA.

That's okay, that's their job. I'll concede that we have the right to enter any Latin American country we please and tell them exactly who their leaders should be and what kind of government they should have. I mean, after all, we're neighbors. We've got the nicest house on the block. We have to make sure the neighbor's lawns are well-tended so the property values don't go down. But fair is fair. If we can send agents to our Latin American neighbors, why can't they send agents here?

Let's say we got a little American town called Smallville, and they don't like their mayor. The rumor around the barbershop is Mayor Brown gave kickbacks to the City Council to change the zoning laws so the mayor's construction company can build the new mall. Smallville isn't pleased, but the election doesn't come around for a couple years. Okay. Enter the Latin American country: let's call it El Dorado.

The El Dorado armed propaganda team is cruising around America in large used station wagons, sort of like traveling salesmen, going door to door with their message of peace, fairness and bullets.

First stop: the Smallville barbershop. The agents of El Dorado assure the barber that the submachine guns and C-4 plastique aren't meant for the barbershop, but the mayor's house. If the barber doesn't become persuaded that shooting Mayor Brown full of holes is the proper solution to civic corruption, they'll go ahead and shoot the barber as an example to others, then surround Smallville and broadcast messages of cheer and solidarity, alternating with bursts of submachine-gun fire.

Soon the town will be behind them 100 percent. They shoot the mayor, the city council, blow up the mall, the hardware store, the Piggly Wiggly, install the barbershop survivors in key positions and drive on to the next town. They're sort of like the Lone Ranger. The survivors will realize, after they've rebuilt their homes, that the goals of El Dorado are the goals of Smallville: God, homeland and democracy.

This is an idea whose time has come: a swap meet of spies. It'll put some spice in American life and give us a firsthand taste of disinformation and termination. It's just a scenario, understand. Smallville needn't worry. *Red Dawn* aside, it can't happen over here. It will always happen over there. And I'm keeping my eyes open at Walden Books for the *CIA Assassination Manual*. It ought to sell like hot cakes.

In the mall, 10/17/84

Waxing Poetic

If I have any regrets about my life—and with my personality I'd better—it would probably be the lack of an elegant prose style. If there were any takers I might give my soul to produce a stately flow of prose like Nabokov or John Cheever. I had a prose style in college, but the plain truth is, I *needed* a prose style then, to cover up my ignorance of the subject at hand. The real world doesn't need a prose style, all the real world wants is copy, material, product.

We've lost a lot over the years. Remember when movies weren't rated? Before we had G, PG, R and X, people actually used to read reviews and make up their own minds about a movie. Now there's just a glance at the ad. If it's G or X, kids won't be caught dead at them. I suppose the ratings system was developed so people wouldn't waste time finding out what a movie's about, but if people are that short of time, they shouldn't waste it at the movies anyway. Movie ratings are just one more stupid system to keep people from thinking. And what happened to Cub Scouts? When I was a kid, we made little sewing baskets for Mom out of popsicle sticks, nowadays kids just want to see Tom Cruise with his shirt off, and Mom's left alone with Dad, wishing Clark Gable was still alive.

There's so much we lose as the years go by. We lose buttons in the morning, socks in the laundry, pens, books and records to our so-called friends, phone numbers in the other pants, we lose our hearts to our lovers, our lovers to our friends, our friends to the changing times. If you own a ten-speed bike it's gonna get stolen. Same with your car stereo system. We lose our jobs, our faith in humanity, our wallets, and watches, youth, memory and minds. Some things we're glad to lose, like the Mr. Microphone we got for Christmas and the hideous tie. Quincy's off the air, thank God, and Dial-A-Porn's days are numbered.

But we still have situation comedies with social implications. We still have psychoanalysis, fluorescent lights, and quadruplex movie theaters. And whither Greenie stickum caps? Whither the 10-cent comic book? Whither Audie Murphy and Randolph Scott? Whither the girl with red hair who sat in front of me in my seventh-grade geography class? My Mom still has the paperweight with the picture of me in my Cub Scout uniform, slightly smeared with plaster-of-paris, but I never made it past my bear badge. Microwaves are getting bigger. Soon all the telephones will be shaped like cartoon animals. Soon smoking will be a capital crime. And the golden years are gone, gone like the snows of yesteryear. Mm. That's good writing.

On the bus, 3/5/84

SNAPSHOTS

Fool on the Hill Here's the picture: on the day Marilyn Monroe died, on a small rolling hill in the Midwest somewhere, a boy stands sweating. This boy will grow up to write the very fine preceding sentence, but on this day the world of grown-ups seems as distant as the prairie spread below him.

He had heard bad news from the lips of Paul Harvey: Marilyn Monroe had died in California. California, where the snows never fall. Where women stroll in bare-naked parades. Where strippers strip and beatniks bongo, actions not possible in the Midwest. The boy labored under the delusion that good sex was possible only in California. He didn't know what good sex was.

He had seen cats mate. Sex seemed to cause cats a great deal of pain. Dogs mated reluctantly, with a confused look, as if they had surrendered to something beyond their control.

The boy had come with his family for a picnic in what is called a "rest area," a small oasis of green off the black strip of highway, in the middle of a prairie scorched brown by August heat. The boy had walked up the hill to brood while his father swatted horseflies and tried to get the coals going.

If you could see this photograph you would see, in the fuzzy distance, a missile silo. In a rectangle of gravel smaller than a suburban lawn, the missile silo squatted like a septic tank, surrounded by a chain-link fence topped with barbed wire.

The boy thought the missile silo was the price the Midwest paid for the pop-culture dreams of a nation, dreams that did not include the Midwest. The Midwest consumed culture made for them in California, while its own culture slowly disappeared: the family, the farm, the small town. . . .

So the boy stood sweating on that hill, thinking about culture, sex and bombs. And that is what his mother snapped on the day Marilyn Monroe died.

Dad with Auto Parts Calendar, 1958 What we have here is a black-and-white picture of a woman in a bikini, reclining on a diving board above a clear pool. The woman has long dark hair, which frames a wide mouth full of white even teeth. She is gently holding a lug wrench the size of a leg. She holds it at a slight distance from her body, the way some people hold a child, or maybe the way Johnny Carson holds a wild animal. The woman's attitude toward the lug wrench could be either of those attitudes. Her smile reveals nothing.

My father is posing next to this calendar. He too is smiling—a half-smile; the kind of smile he would get when men told dirty jokes. He didn't like dirty jokes. But he smiled to be polite, and to persuade these men to buy his products.

This picture was taken by a garage mechanic in the summer of 1958. My father had a job that summer selling auto parts. I went with him once. We drove to small towns all around the state, from garage to garage. That summer was my introduction to sex in popular culture. I saw naked women on calendars, naked women on matchbooks, naked women on playing cards. I heard punch lines to jokes I didn't understand. You can see from my father's face he didn't understand them either, but his misunderstanding was of a different nature.

Hallowe'en, 1959 That's me in there under the aluminum foil. I put an old garbage can over my head, poked two eye holes in it, then wrapped foil around cardboard tubes and boxes, put it all on my body as best I could, and posed, embarrassed, for my mother, who seemed to think I was cute. I had tried to look like Robby the Robot (a.k.a. Tobor the Robot). I had failed.

Two years later, Robby the Robot was to play an important role in my first sexual fantasy. He and Gort (from *The Day the Earth Stood Still)* captured me on my way home from school, and deposited me in a steel windowless room with Karen

Tvedt. The better to observe earthling mating habits, they stripped us naked and forced us to make a twelve-year-old's version of love. As with animals, the sexuality was beyond our control.

My fantasies were informed as much by science-fiction movies as by *Playboy*. The ubiquitous Cold War even reached its cold fingers into my libido, if space aliens are considered subliminal stand-ins for Commies.

I think I was twelve when I first saw the famous *Playboy* photograph of Marilyn Monroe. What I felt when I gazed at this picture was not lust so much as vertigo. She seemed real in a way not intended by the photographer. Norma Jean: a lonely brunette lost in a disguise.

Playboy was a magazine from another planet. *Playboy* was why the state I lived in had missile silos. *Playboy* and Disneyland, *Bonanza* and Huntley and Brinkley—that was the real world. We were the Martians.

My First Girlfriend's Mother, with Bourbon My girlfriend's sister snapped this one. My girlfriend's mother's red hair wasn't real, but the rest of her seemed to be. She was the kind of woman who likes to think of herself as bawdy. She was a registered nurse. She had a great laugh and she laughed a lot. She also drank a lot. She told me once that she'd been married three times (though my girlfriend said four). In the time I knew her, I never saw her date anybody. On the night this picture was taken, she told me a story.

During World War II, on the East Coast, she fell in love with a bomber pilot. On their wedding night, she said, he had to fly away. He couldn't tell her where he was flying, but he told her to go to the hospital roof at midnight, and watch.

Though the city was blacked out that night, when she explained the romance of the moment to the kindhearted custodian, he let her go up. Up on the hospital roof, she could hear the bombers before she could see them, and on that moonless night she could barely see them at all. She could only see the pinpoint lights of their wings as they flew in formation.

As she leaned back to watch them pass overhead, the lights

of the wings flicked off, then on again. She realized with a sudden thrill that a squadron of bombers had just winked at her. Then they passed slowly from her sight, and she never saw her husband again.

Five years later she met husband number three (or four), gave birth to my girlfriend, then her sister, then divorced the jerk.

Unlike most heavy drinkers she only told a good story once. I liked her a lot better than my girlfriend. That's probably why we broke up.

Suicide Blonde No, I didn't take any of these pictures. I hate photography. This picture was taken when I was a bartender, snapped by the art student at the end of the bar, who'd spent the day taking Polaroids of bicycle spokes for a sculpture project.

The subject of this photograph is one of the waitresses. She's french-inhaling a menthol cigarette and trying to look mean. She called the color of her shag "suicide blonde."

If business was slow and she was high enough, she'd pull up her blouse and show you the button-shaped midriff scar where Johnny had shot her with a .22. Or she'd show you the long scar on her calf where Joe the speed freak had cut her. She'd pull back her hair so you could see the tiny scar on her ear where Billy Reed had ripped away the gold hoop.

She had a lot of scars and every one had a story. She thought her stories were funny. She thought her scars were funny. When I got fired from that job, she had a new boyfriend, a guy named Smoky. She thought Smoky was funny. I don't know why. He was a skinny nervous guy who never laughed at all.

In the long years since this photograph was taken, I'll bet she's gathered a lot of stories. I'll bet she thinks they're all funny.

Lib The guy told me this was a Polaroid of his wife. She's naked. Her expression, meant to represent desire, has always looked like pain to me. This guy wanted to send the picture to *Penthouse* but he didn't have the brainpower to figure out how. He thought it might be illegal for one thing, and he didn't know if developers could make a copy from a Polaroid. He was more embarrassed about seeming ignorant to some drugstore film developer than showing a snapshot of his naked wife to a stranger in a bar.

"What's your wife think?" I asked him. He said his wife had just left him and taken the kids with her. He tried to sell me the picture for five bucks. I told him I wasn't interested. When he left, he left the Polaroid on the bar, half-buried under a pile of loose change. I've spent a long time staring at that picture. If the world is made for pleasure, is this how we fill our leisure time?

Preteen Angel I'm standing up in the front seat of a 1953 blue Ford sedan. You can't see the color in the picture, but I remember the car well. I don't look happy. My grandmother, whose face cannot be seen, has just told me to sit down. I don't want to sit down. I liked to stand up in the front seat as we drove, my eyes level with my father's, my back against the front seat, my knees locked—the small king of a moving kingdom.

"You won't always be that small," she told me.

One of the things I didn't like about my grandmother was her common sense. I didn't like common sense. Nobody likes common sense. Nobody wants to know the future.

In the attic, 3/25/85

ODDS AND ENDS

Out with the old, in with the new. Time to clear off the desk, sweep away the old ideas, make room for new ideas. I never got around, for example, to my exposé on the counterfeit Cabbage Patch-doll ring. That's probably a good thing.

I never got to my in-depth probe of Bruce Springsteen—not him or his music, but the critical attitude toward him. I can't tell you how many columns I've read about Bruce Springsteen, none of them about his songs. No, most writers admire The Boss because he's such a hard worker. This is a critical slant I'd never seen before—nothing about talent or anything like that, just descriptions of his sweat and the backstage aroma of Vicks Vapo-Rub. I guess it finally had to happen. Bruce Springsteen has taken over Sammy Davis, Jr.'s, title of Hardest-Working Man in Show Business.

I don't know if he wanted the title, but he's got it. While we're on this subject, I wanted to do a piece on that MTV contest: the winner got to be a Bruce Springsteen roadie for two weeks. If you won this contest you got to lug heavy equipment around then drive all night to the next gig. Hey, what a prize. Enter me in that one.

And this counterfeit Cabbage Patch-doll ring. That must be a problem for somebody.

And in the "Life's Little Mysteries" department, I wanted to explore the fake antique look you see in certain hamburger joints. You know, they have pictures on the stick-em wallpaper of ladies with parasols, strolling about, or riding those old-time bicycles. All the plastic is made to look like wrought iron, and the lamps all look like gas lamps. In a hamburger joint? What are they trying to tell us? These are Victorian hamburgers? None of the underpaid teens behind the counter could answer this one for me.

Another poser: If the book based on a hit movie is called a novelization, what do you call the person that writes this book? A novelizator? A novelizer? A film-analog-concept coordinator? Okay, it's not a big problem, but it bugs me.

I never got around to that piece on the counterfeit Cabbage Patch dolls. I tried, but every time I started to write it my flesh would crawl.

I'm grateful in a backhand way for the movie *2010* because it affords me this brief opportunity to say that the original *2001: A Space Odyssey* is the most boring movie of all time. How people can say they admire this pretentious solemn and philosophically silly excuse for a movie is really beyond me.

And speaking of movies, why didn't they rerelease *Eraserhead* for Christmas instead of making David Lynch do *Dune*? Or better yet, why didn't somebody produce *Eraserhead II*? I'm not the first to remark on the amazing similarity between Don Knotts and Mick Jagger, but did anybody ever notice how much the Eraserhead baby looked like E.T.? Of course you didn't. That's why you have me around. And E.T. looks an awful lot like a counterfeit Cabbage Patch doll.

Till next time, remember: getting rid of welfare because of welfare cheats is like getting rid of convenience stores because people rob them. How can water beading be good in one commercial if high absorbency is good in another? I don't know.

I don't know a lot of things. I don't know why my treatment for a new game show, *Celebrity Terrorism*, got turned down by all the major networks. I don't know why *Entertainment Tonight* hasn't moved into a twenty-four-hour-a-day format. I don't know why we haven't named the MX missile as our fifty-first state. I don't know why Larry Flynt didn't get elected president. I don't know why we don't have more all-night TV movies and fewer books about cats. I don't know why they don't make sharkskin pajamas. I'd buy them. I don't know why Richard Simmons is famous, or why *Love*

Boat is still on the air. I don't know how you can tell if a Cabbage Patch doll is counterfeit. Maybe there's a way of measuring the wrinkles. The answers, my friend, are blowing in the wind. Don't ask me. I'm just the weatherman who knows which way the wind blows. I don't have the answers, just a job. My job is sneering. It's a tough job, but somebody's gotta do it. And let me clue you, pals and gals, sneering doesn't pay enough. I gotta go.

Feeling wistful, 1/1/85

AFTERWORD

"M. Shoales: *Nouvelle critique ou nouvelle imposture?*"
(M. Shoales: New Criticism or New Fraud?)
by Jean-Claude De Valery

(*Trans. Note:* This first appeared in *Le Monde,* March 28, 1982. It was translated by Ian Shoales and reprinted without permission.)

To place in the Established Order the fear of its own symbols is to embrace the Established Order. This paradox has happily been lost on M. Shoales, who persists with his "opinions" that bring expression *(esprit)* and reaction into new realms of juxtaposition. The inferred decadence in his poses is the residuum of revolutionary hysteria meeting the cold pragmatism of the (Marcusean) dictatorial insanity. Only I know what this means.

But it is amusing to see M. Shoales give his aural proofs of the subjugation of expression to the architecture-in-motion that creates that sequence of sounds into a form which the record industry calls a "pop-song." But his gaze *(regard),* as seemingly inscrutable as the Sphinx, falls on the American musics no less than other manifestations of the Bourgeois: movies *(cinéma),* television, drugs, disease—he exposes the tiny ironies of society's structures of control. His so-called "critical response" *(esprit)* is a purely empirical reaction, a useless yet brave discourse lost in the microcosm of popular culture (see my own *Plaisir de Rock et Roll* for the display of consumption in the correct context: the death of literature and the despair of the learned in the face of that death).

Why continue? From the great Sade to the reactionary Sartre the narrative of critical response is a pure unbroken line. While M. Shoales does nothing to interrupt this line, his informed intelligence addresses itself admirably to the trivia of the taxonomic grid of the hermetic world of popular culture. But what of Nietzsche, Van Gogh, Artaud? The world must justify itself before the madness of those it imprisons.

So I sit and drink my green tea here at the École, where I occupy a small seat on the margins of the university system. Perhaps that is as it should be. I am a writer of small essays *(feuilletoniste)*, which written drop into the void of history as pearls into the pond which held the gaze *(regard)* of Narcissus. I do not write them; rather they are written by me. You do not read them; rather they are read by you. I do not accept the check; rather the check is mailed to me. Where is my check? The check is in the mail?

ABOUT DUCK'S BREATH

Founded in a cloud of dim purpose and vague desire on a wintry Iowa City night in 1975, Duck's Breath Mystery Theatre retains its original membership and sheer sense of survival. The troupe—Bill Allard, Dan Coffey, Merle Kessler, Leon Martell and Jim Turner—has careened from coast-to-coast via live shows and National Public Radio's "All Things Considered" and "Morning Edition."

Collectively and chaotically, the five have earned everything from critical raves to confused smiles with their menagerie of flying non sequiturs, sophisticated slapstick, odd costumes and grotesque facial expressions. Onstage incidents have included hundreds of sketches and dozens of one-acts (including *A Cliff Note's Hamlet, Gonad the Barbarian* and *Senseless Cruelty: A New Western*), while evidence abounds that the troupe screenplay, *Zarda: Cow From Hell!* may be the greatest movie never made.

Now based in San Francisco, the group has served as staff writers for the Nickelodeon kids cable TV series, *Out of Control,* produced its own radio series "Homemade Radio" on some 170 stations and allowed Ian Shoales (Merle Kessler) room to sneer on ABC-TV's *Nightline, That Was The Week That Was,* NPR and elsewhere. A daily dose of absurdity, "Ask Dr. Science," pontificates on American Public Radio network stations, and numerous alleged cassettes and pending media events have staved off moral bankruptcy and illicit public behavior by the troupe.

For more information on Ian Shoales and Duck's Breath Mystery Theatre, simply and painlessly join the Duck's Breath mailing list. Harass us at your convenience:

> Duck's Breath
> PO Box 22513
> San Francisco, CA   94122

INDEX

Dogs

Employment, Self

Fear, 20

Joe

Kessler, Merle

underrated writer, not mentioned in text

Lists

of bad things in the sixties, 14–16
of contemporary horrors, 21–22
of cute things, 26–27
of humanistic images, 114–15
of likes, 69
of nonexistent television programs, 148–49
of things to avoid in college, 81–82
of things to avoid at temp jobs, 46–47
of white lies, 30–31
of women, 101–2

Mom

advice of, 46, 107
and camera, 169–73
and eviction of Ian Shoales, 17, 52
and fridge, 11–19

Norgaard, Miss, 12, 40, 41

Ramones, The, 18, 68, 74, 126

Rock-and-Roll Novel, 1,500-PAGE, 47, 91

See Rider

See WHAT YOU DONE DONE

Shoales, Ian

ant farm of, 79
girlfriends of, 17, 62–64, 74, 101, 105–6, 109–10,
110–11, 112–13, 157, 171, 172
likes of, 68–70
opinions of, 11–176
utopian visions of, 73–74

Teens

friendly, 24
sexual role models of, 128
spending habits of, 129
stupid, 150–51
terrified, 150–51
with a brain, 18

Thanks, Many

to Steve Baker, Brad Bunnin, and the Ducks
to Peter Breslow, Alex Chadwick, Rich Harris,